What Others Are Saying ...

Bill Bohline's stories provide hope for anyone who simply wants to live a more fulfilling life. I was inspired both at a personal and professional level.

DR. LISA L. SNYDER, *superintendent*
Lakeville (Minn.) Area Public Schools

What an unusual book. Humor. Tragedy. Theology. Reality. But most of all, *hope.*

Some people wonder if Christian faith really works. Here is the resounding answer of "Yes!"

DR. LEITH ANDERSON, *president*
National Association of Evangelicals

I LOVE this book! Why? Because it's about life, the one thing none of us asked to get into and have to die to get out of. Bill points us to life so rich and powerful that it triumphs everything.

REGGIE MCNEAL, *national speaker and author*

Bill is a very gifted communicator who has the ability to tell a story that makes Scripture real, applies to my life, makes me laugh and makes me cry. In this book, Bill's gift shines, and Jesus is lifted up.

KRISTI GRANER, *director*
Dare to Believe Ministries

As the daily grind and unexpected circumstances begin to overshadow our Sunday devotions, this book sheds light on how to find God's love.

JOEL MANBY, *president and CEO*
Herschend Family Entertainment (theme parks)

Bill Bohline masterfully weaves humor and Scripture to remind us of a personal God who yearns to be involved with our lives. A fun read ... but also a real boost to spiritual growth!

SUSIE SHELLENBERGER
Speaker; founding editor of Brio *magazine*

Pastor Bill's powerful, faith-filled stories of God at work challenge us all to expect God's impact and to wait upon the Lord seven days a week, not just on Sunday.... Humorous, captivating, emotionally gripping.

JUDGE DAVID KNUTSON
Dakota County, Minn.

This book quickly awakens our minds, touches our hearts, shows us courage in the face of fears, and brings light to the darkest path.

PAT MOE, *pastor for care ministries*
Hosanna! Lutheran Church

Great humor (often at Bill's own expense) combine here with unflinching straight talk about the best and toughest parts of life. Throughout the book, we get constant, compelling stories of God's transformation.

JOHN CROSBY, *senior pastor*
Christ Presbyterian Church, Edina, Minn.

Pastor Bill's unique writing style will keep you reading (and laughing!), but his message will keep you hungry for more. You'll discover the same God you worship for an hour on Sunday showing up in the details of your Monday.

MARY J. NELSON, *author of* Grace for Each Hour

It's Sunday, *but Monday's Comin'*

Finding Faith
for the Rest of the Week

Bill Bohline

with Dean Merrill

For more information, go to: www.mondayscomin.com
or contact: Hosanna! Books, 9600 163rd St., Lakeville, MN 55044. Phone: (952) 898-9137.

Unless otherwise indicated, all Scripture quotations are taken from the Holy Bible, New Living Translation, copyright © 1996, 2004, 2007 by Tyndale House Foundation. Used by permission of Tyndale House Publishers Inc., Carol Stream, Illinois 60188. All rights reserved.

In chapters 4 and 11, certain names and other identifications have been changed due to the sensitive issues involved. The essence of the narratives, however, is true to what actually occurred.

Printed in the United States of America

Contents

Introduction

IS GOD RELIABLE?

Today is my birthday. My nice Facebook friends are saying stuff like "Happy birthday, young man" or "This next year is going to be the best ever." My other friends (why didn't I click on *ignore?*) are congratulating me on qualifying for Social Security, which is absurd at my age.

Anyway, as I was running this morning (just to see if I still could), a couple of random thoughts came to me. I was laboring on a gentle incline that seemed steeper than usual when my brain piped up: *You've never been this old before.* Seems self-evident, but it can also be self-defeating if you dwell on it. Which I couldn't, because this thought came along six strides later: *You'll never be this young again.* I was afraid of what other thoughts might come if I kept climbing that mountain, so I quickly turned around and jogged back to the cabin, where a nice hammock awaited.

It's amazing how our random thoughts can affect us. One minute it's a blue-sky day, and then you realize you have to pay bills today. For the longest time you're adoring your baby (or grand-child)—and suddenly you realize you're the one who has to change that diaper. You start reading this book with great expectations, but in the second paragraph you remember, "Hey, I know the guy who wrote this, and he can't even write a grocery list."

Our thoughts affect our mood, energy level, confidence, outlook, hopes, joy, waist measurement, everything. So, when I hear a good thought, I tend to hang on to it.

I heard John Ortberg, one of my favorite pastor-authors, speak recently, and something he said is still taped onto the front wall of my mind: **"God never changes, but when he shows up, it changes everything."** I like that thought. I don't want God to be like the Dow Jones. *Well, the market is reacting to the price of chili beans today and is down 172 points.* I don't want God to be like some friend saying, "Oh, was it today that we were going to have lunch?"

I want him to be reliable, consistent, faithful, powerful, unyielding, stable, calm, and above all, engaged with my daily life. That's not too much to ask. It's a big job, but he's a big God. In the Bible he is described as a rock and a fortress, a protector and a shield, the unending source of peace, strength, joy, and blessing. Now we're talking. "Trust in the Lord with all your heart; do not depend on your own understanding. Seek his will in all you do and he will direct your paths."[1] That's the way I want it to be. That's the way I want him to be.... So I'm all on board with the concept.

But here's the deal: I want that to be, I *need* that to be more than just a thought. I want that to be my daily reality. I have lots of good thoughts that never become a reality:

- I have always thought the Minnesota Vikings are going to win a Super Bowl. Then in 2009, along came Brett Favre. Super Bowl parties were planned all over the state (and not just to watch the commercials). When the New Orleans Saints beat us in the NFC title game, I went into a major sulk.

- For twelve years I have thought my GMC Jimmy would make it to 250,000 miles. It's sitting at 180,000, but last week the transmission started clunking, the AC went out, and a horrible hailstorm beat up on it. Bye-bye, Jimmy.

- All my life I thought I was going to be tall.

Obviously some thoughts aren't ever going to become reality.

But the thought about God being active in my life is different. For me to trust him, follow him, worship him – major stuff like that – I need to see God, to know God, as more than just a thought. More than a major mover in history.

That's what this book is about. I want the God of the Bible to square up with my reality, my daily experience. In the Bible, God shows up every-where. Like Regis Philbin or Betty White. He helps people, heals them, counsels them, comforts them, confronts them, and ultimately changes them. He does make everything different. Isn't that what you really want out of God?

Several years ago Tony Campolo wrote a book entitled *It's Friday, but Sunday's Comin'*. He wrote about how we live in a Friday world with pain, grief, disease, separation, fear—you get the idea. Good Friday was the darkest day in history, and hope seemed to be extinguished. But then came Easter. The Devil was defeated, light pierced the darkness, the gates to eternity were thrown open, and hope was restored. Campolo's book points us to the top of the mountain, where there is victory and celebration.

I'm simply saying that beyond that mountain there is probably another valley. But the thing is, God doesn't just dwell on the mountaintop. He's familiar with the valley, and his desire is not just to give us what we need, but to give us himself. The God we worship on Sunday is the God we can walk with on Monday. In fact, that's where we get to know him best. That's what I want to show you.

Listen, I do live by faith. The roots go down pretty deep, in fact. I'm not saying I simply have deep *thoughts* about God. I am saying that the roots of my faith go way down into the marvelous soil of his love for me and this world. But honestly (and I shouldn't tell you this, so please don't mention this to anyone in my church), my faith needs a little Miracle-Gro now and then. A good story of God's intervention, an "aha" moment, even a few goosebumps, a tear or two. Then I feel and know his presence. My trust grows stronger, and the light of my faith burns a little brighter. My thoughts and hopes about God are *realized.*

In this book I'm going to showcase for you how God shows up on more than just Sundays. We'll look at a Bible story or two in each area to see what *God did.* Then I'll tell you a story or two about real-life people to illustrate what *God does.* I hope you will come to see that the God of the Bible is still in business, doing what he has always done. His desires and plans are the same, his power is not diminished, and he has a good handle on things.

When God shows up, it changes everything. That's more than a good thought. It can be your reality—seven days a week.

1

MORE THAN CANDLES AND BELLS

"What happens in Vegas stays in Vegas." It's a dumb thought that seems to have a half-life a little like plutonium. It won't go away, and nobody is sure how to bury it.

The problem is that it seems to have a fairly direct application within the church. What happens on Sunday stays on Sunday. There is a dramatic discrepancy between what we do on Sunday and what we do on Monday.

On Sunday we worship, on Monday we work. On Sunday we bow down, on Monday we bear down. On Sunday we smile and pass the peace, on Monday we smile and give others a piece of our minds. On one level this makes sense (not the part about giving others a piece of your mind – they don't want it, and you should probably hang onto it). What makes sense is that our behavior in church is different than our behavior in the cubicle. Fine. You don't want people taking up an offering in the office or shouting "Hallelujah," except for Friday at 5:00.

But here's the root issue: Our faith tends to falter when our Sunday God and our Monday God aren't the same. On Sunday God is high, holy, wise, loving, forgiving, and in control. He's on his throne with the whole company of heaven singing "Holy, Holy, Holy," and we get to join in. On Monday the singing has stopped and God can seem more like a loving but distant grandpa who knew a lot of things but has a tendency to doze off now and again. It makes me nervous to describe God somewhat like myself, but I'm trying to make a point here.

I much prefer for things to be in alignment. I like it when something works like the warranty says it will. I like it when promises and practices are the same. I like it when my tires don't wobble, and I like it that two and two always equal four. Nice. So of course I want my Sunday God and my Monday God to be one and the same. No differences. No limited warranties or disclaimers for me. Alignment.

Bethlehem Boy

For a long time it seemed to me that things were out of alignment. I grew up at Bethlehem. Not the one where Jesus was born and the Motel 6 innkeeper forgot to leave the light on. Bethlehem was a healthy little Lutheran church on the north side of Minneapolis. Growing up in Minneapolis, you were either Lutheran or Catholic or Other. Not many people wanted to be Other, so most people wound up on one of the two big-league teams. The Catholics always seemed to outnumber us. Their families had more babies, something the Pope ordered, we thought. And, by the way, why didn't we have a Pope? Some Big Shot making all the rules and wearing fancy clothes.

Like I was saying, I grew up at Bethlehem, which was a church with a bell tower, stained-glass windows, a pipe organ, and red carpet right down the middle leading up to the altar. When you were old enough, you got to be an acolyte. That's a church word for candle lighter. You had to show up early (fifteen minutes *before* the service!), put on a scratchy white robe, walk out in front of everybody *with the pastor* and light all the candles while everybody watched. I was so short I couldn't always tell if they were lit, so the pastor would give me hand signals to move on to the next candle. Then you had to sit up front on these wooden thrones while the pastor led worship and preached a long sermon. I was never sure what I had done to deserve this punishment.

Our pastor was Dr. A.W. Arthur. Not A & W— our Bethlehem was no root beer stand. Most people called him Dr. Arthur, but if you got to know him real well you could call him Abby. I think I was seventeen before I knew what the A.W. stood for: Abner Wentworth. Maybe his mother wanted a girl. Dr. Arthur preached without any notes, and this made a huge impression on people. I thought if he had notes he could shorten things up a little.

At Bethlehem I went to Sunday school, where Violet Larson would sing "Jesus Loves Me" every week and the dogs in the neighborhood would all howl. She wore her hair in a bun forever and was single. I did wonder if she had let her hair down a man might have taken notice. Violet was the Sun-day school superin-tendent (sort of a mini-Pope), and Wil-bur Anderson was the guy

> **Dr. Arthur preached without any notes, and this made a huge impression on people. I thought if he had notes he could shorten things up a little.**

sentenced to teach the boys. He looked a little like a basset hound and could sing only two notes, in no particular order. But when he sang "Jesus Loves Me" the neighborhood dogs settled back down.

He's the guy who first got us clued in on Moses, David, Samson (and Delilah), Jesus, the Pharisees, the Sadducees, and the Wannabes. Wilbur sure seemed to know a lot. And what he didn't know, Dr. Arthur would cover in the next sermon.

Not only did we go to Bethlehem, but my mom was the parish secretary! Seriously. She worked there, and so we were doing church stuff all the time. Sometimes the pastors would come over to our house for dinner and act fairly normal. I just assumed they should be in the office working on their next sermon or spending some time in prayer for us members (sometimes called "parishioners," which sounds like a cult to me).

Plus, on Saturday nights, we would take a bath and get our fingernails cut so we were sanitized for church. And then my dad would get out *Hurlburt's Story of the Bible* and we would have a Bible story before "Bonanza" came on. So the same Bible heroes Wilbur was telling us about were talked about in our house – with pictures too. I knew exactly what Samson looked like when he destroyed that heathen temple. He could have been governor of California. Daniel looked real cool walking around with those lions, and Jesus seemed to be fond of children.

Plus, we had a board game called Going to Jerusalem. You had to answer Bible trivia questions and could move your guy along the board through towns like Capernaum, Bethany, Duluth, and Fargo, and the first guy to Jerusalem won. I usually got stuck in Caesarea Philippi, which I thought was a pizza parlor just outside Jerusalem.

What I'm trying to tell you is this: I was in and around church all my life. I knew God and his guys. I knew about Mary Magdalene too, but I didn't think we were supposed to talk about her because she had issues. I also knew pastors, memorized Bible verses to get out of confirmation, said prayers, and generally thought we were pretty good players on the Lutheran team. It did bother me that the Catholic services were shorter, and they didn't seem to get as many "stewardship" sermons (you know, the money talk). But all in all, the Lutheran team ran a good show (particularly on Sundays), and we as a family were insiders.

Low Expectations

Now, shouldn't all of this give me a huge advantage toward being a faithful follower of Christ, a faith-filled person? Yes and no. Yes, I was immersed ... (I need to say a word here about immersion baptism. This is where you dunk the whole person under water with their clothes on and they come up sputtering and smiling. We were against it growing up, because that's what the Baptist team did and a few Pentecostals. It's interesting that the Lutheran and Catholic teams agreed on this play. You dress the baby up in a little angel gown – even the boys – and you gather around a font and, at the right time, you splash a *little* water on the baby's head three times. This is usually when the baby wakes up and starts screaming and the dad starts sweating and the pastor talks louder trying to wrap things up. Frankly, I was always jealous of the dunkers, because it seemed like a full-bodied experience. So now we do immersion baptisms at our church when requested, but please don't tell anyone. I will disclose a few other things to you in this book, but they must remain just between you and me. Confidentiality is a big thing for me, unless it's about my sister).

Like I was saying, I was immersed ... in church language, church culture, and church ritual. It was all part of the fabric of our family life. You would call us believers. Good ones. We knew what to believe and why. We practiced and prayed. My dad sang in the choir, and Mom printed the bulletins. We had reason to hope for a good outcome when we died.

But here's the rub: Our Sunday life, with all that believing and good behaving, should have led to pretty high results on Monday, even an occasional whopper experience or encounter with God. No reason to think God was confined within the covers of a book, no matter how holy it was or stuck in all that stained glass, even though it really did catch the sunlight. But out of all that church immersion there really never came any high expectations. In fact, even though nobody ever really said so, it just seemed like we were to keep our expectations kinda low, so as not to be disappointed.

It's not that God couldn't still do his big stuff, but why should he? He didn't have to prove himself, and we had no right to put him on the spot. Not only that, but if anybody did claim to have some kind of encounter with God, well, we didn't really celebrate it or talk much about it. We tried to explain it in psychological or gastronomical terms. Stress, fatigue, Domino's.

My mother was a bit unusual, in that she told of a born-again experience when she was about thirty years old. She did grow up in Arkansas, so nobody expected her to be quite as stable as all of us Minnesotans, who root for the Vikings and eat fish cooked in lye. She just knelt down by the bathtub one night and cried and told the Lord she couldn't go on the way things were and he

> *It just seemed like we were to keep our church expectations kinda low, so as not to be disappointed.*

would have to do something about it. So, he showed up and said he would.

It was personal and powerful. She was never the same person after that. From that day on, she was glad she had a personal relationship with Jesus Christ, and she knew she was going to heaven. Which is where she is today. As Lutherans, we thought she should be a little less certain about her eternal destination. After all, we are both saints and sinners and, we thought that depending on which day you die, you could be on the wrong side of the "and" in that scheme of things. I have come around to her way of believing – more on that later.

It's just that a lot of people waited for my mom to "get over" her experience. We weren't "experience" people. Keep the expectations low, and keep the experiences to yourself. We could read the Bible stories and sing the hymns on Sunday, but Monday never really followed Sunday in terms of expectations and experiences. We were believers, but we weren't about to be fanatics.

I have to think the Sunday-Monday disconnect is much harder for those of us brought up in the faith. For those not exposed to faith or church, Sunday is just a bonus Saturday, and Monday is what life is really all about, making a living.

In my mind this is where the church has done more harm than good. The message that we often get in church is that that's where the action is. If you would sing in a choir, get on a committee, teach Sunday school, and *give a little more,* well, then God would be pleased and you'll be a little closer to heaven. But you have to come back next week and do it again or heaven's door will start to close. At times the church is like a football team that studies the play book, listens to the coach, huddles up every Sunday and then never runs a play during the week. When that keeps happening, then the playbook becomes a dusty manual of what once was or could have been, and Sunday seems a l o n g way from Monday.

But I know of many people who are running the plays on Monday. They are praying with people, feeding and clothing people, visiting them in hospitals and prisons, speaking life not death, love not hate, light not darkness, and faith not fear. And they are bumping into God all over the place. He's out there, and it's like Acts 29 is getting written right now. (I'll just write this for my good friend, Frank. Acts is the book in the Bible that describes all the wonderful, powerful things the church accomplished in the early days because believers *practiced* their faith on Mondays. The book only has 28 chapters so far, but chapter 29 is just as amazing). Some of those stories are in this book.

Outside the Box

Somehow I wound up going into the ministry (that's another story for a different chapter) and started a church. In the early days of that effort, we had to determine who our target audience was. Were we going for traditional Lutherans or some of those contemporary types? Did we hope to pick a few off of the Catholic team? Did we want to go for a few unchurched, even though that was the job of the television evangelists and we really wouldn't know what to do with them?

So the debate ensued. In the midst of the debate we did a wild, reckless thing. It could have gotten us thrown out of the club if it became widely known. We took our staff to a leadership conference at Willow Creek Community Church in South Barrington, Illinois. This is a monster, nondenominational (Father, forgive them) church in the outskirts of Chicago. No pews, no stained-glass windows, no altar, and not a single cross in sight. Unbelievable. The only redeeming factor seemed to be that the senior pastor (the founding pastor) was named Bill. For some reason they were drawing 10,000-12,000 people on a weekend. That's more than a Golden Gopher football game most years. People were coming from all over the country to their conferences to learn some things and to report back to headquarters on any heresy. Lutherans are good at that.

Willow is a "seeker-sensitive" church. Most churches are seeker-insensitive or even seeker-hostile. You show up there and nobody talks to you – they stare, but don't talk. Plus, you can't find the bathrooms, and you feel like you have visited some kind of a foreign embassy. Well, Willow Creek was friendly and had good bathrooms. They had removed all the religious symbols from the building in order to start on level ground with those who were seeking, searching, uncertain about faith matters or church. And they were wildly successful, even though the first night we were there was an Ash Wednesday, and Ash Wednesday was *never even mentioned*. Wait till our bishop hears about that!

Willow Creek's target audience was Unchurched Harry and Unchurched Mary. The leadership conference was a package program on how you could connect with the Harrys and Marys in your community.

Yikes. Our church was about eight years old, and we had a bunch of solid Lutherans showing up. We did talk about "guest speakers," but never about "guest seekers." So, had God shown us something at Willow Creek that would define our future, or should we stick with the assigned program which was good enough for Martin Luther 450 years ago?

Because our church had started with me out there knocking on doors in the neighborhoods, I had a sense of who was in the community. The vast majority back then still had some kind of church experience growing up, but there was never anything really personal about it, much less powerful or life-changing. Church was still on the menu for them, but it wasn't the main course. I'm not suggesting that God was an appetizer. He was certainly one of the boxes you would check on your resume:

   _ x _ Educated

   _ x _ Employed

   _ x _ Vikings fan

   _ x _ God.

He was part of the plan, but not the One with the plan.

So, after lots of discussion and debate and a few laughs, we zeroed in on our target audience: Lukewarm Lutherans and Comatose Catholics. It was fine if a few Passive Presbyterians or Moribund Methodists came along, but we wanted to keep our sights on the big teams. These were great people for whom the whole faith experience was left at the corporate level. You worship as a group, confess sins as a group (except for some of the Catholics on Saturday night before they went out drinking), you maybe sang in the choir or got yourself on a committee. These are all good things, but they can keep God at quite a distance. And on Monday, these folks weren't talking about God, they were talking about which teams were going to make the Final Four.

We had to figure out how best to connect with the Lukewarm Lutherans and the Comatose Catholics. For them, faith was a little pilot light that had never been ignited. So what do you do? Well, we started singing songs that were *not in the hymnal* (remember our confidentiality agreement). I started preaching sermons in a series rather than stand-alone messages week after week. We'd do a series on parenting, marriage, prayer, sex (when I was out of town), finances, and in-laws. People seemed to like that.

We started paying more attention to what our faith was supposed to mean between Sundays. We didn't want to do pop psychology (remember the book *I'm OK, You're OK?*), but we did want our faith to have Monday meaning. The weekends became a little more like a visit to the optometrist and we started to see things more clearly all week long.

Then I took off my clothes. When I'm telling the story of our church to a group, I usually say that just to see if anyone is still listening. Here I wanted to see if you were still reading. What I mean by that is I stopped wearing the white bathrobe that you get when you become a pastor (called an alb) and I also stopped wearing the clerical collar. It's just a little plastic tab thing that keeps rubbing up against your Adam's apple.

Before I took off my clothes, I wrote a paper to the church board explaining why I thought I should try this. It seemed like a huge deal to me. But nobody said boo. So my alb still hangs in my closet. I get it out for skits and anniversaries.

We've done a million other things to make good people connections, but there is one thing that has mattered more than anything else: real-life stories. I stopped presenting myself as the answer man and talked more openly about my shortcomings and the things I wrestled with. It felt good to get out of the pulpit and just stand on a platform in front of people.

Oxygen for the Soul

Even as the church continued to grow, we got closer. It's hard to describe, but there's a special kind of intimacy to be found in candor and vulnerability. It wasn't a gimmick to attract more people—humor and humility have always been attractive.

And another thing happened. We didn't just have a keener sense of each other's presence, but of God's presence as well. God has a great desire to move among his people and not just in church. He does his best work outside the church, where he can surprise us and stretch us and show off.

We all became better at identifying his hand in things and responding to some nudges he might give us. Our expectations began to climb and our anticipation was heightened. It was like every week was going to be an adventure, a little mission trip where God would use us to serve a neighbor or someone in need, right in the house or cubicle next door. We also began to tell our stories – little ones and big ones. As we did, a sense of joy and vitality came over us. Faith moved from being a personal possession to being oxygen for our souls.

Something we always wanted came to be. God was no longer a mystery shrouded in history. He was, well ... God. Knowing and known, loving and loved, powerful but oh so personal. People were healed, marriages were saved, addictions were broken, and hearts were mended – just like in the Bible. And we couldn't wait to tell others.

We can't wait to tell you.

2

SO WHAT'S THE PLAN?

Minnesota is the state with over 10,000 lakes, ponds, and puddles. Plus, the Mighty Mississippi begins in our fine state. You can go almost anywhere by boat ... or nine months of the year, when the lakes are frozen, you can go by snowmobile. When you get tired of that, you move to Phoenix or Fort Myers and send postcards back to your relatives.

The thing is, if you live in Minnesota, you do want to try to enjoy the water. Ten years ago Nancy and I bought a little cabin on Lake Sylvia. I don't know anything about Sylvia, but she must have been a very fine woman because the lake is beautiful and shapely. We had just put our daughter through private college and so had lived in debtors' prison for four years, while she lived in a penthouse dorm room eating free food and skipping classes. We realized that if we could put her through college, we could also actually afford to buy a modest lake cabin. So we did.

The cabin was over sixty-five years old, and everyone who came to visit said it was "cute" or "adorable," which is Scandinavian code for "Well, at least you've got a place." Before we moved in, the bees and bats had already taken up residence in the attic, and we coexisted for ten years. Although one morning we woke up to the swishing sound of a bat flying around our bedroom. Nancy went screaming out of the bedroom and into our bathroom, where she locked the door. I mean, bats have that radar thing going on, but I don't think they can open doors. I put on a football helmet and a snowmobile suit and went back into the bedroom to do battle with the bat. He's soaring with the angels now and probably eating the mosquitoes up there, which is a blessing for all those saints who have already gone through a lot of plagues and stuff.

> *The cabin was over sixty-five years old, and everyone who came to visit said it was "cute" or "adorable," which is Scandinavian code for "Well, at least you've got a place."*

For years we dreamed about having a cabin to ourselves (no bees or bats) and one that we could use all year round. Our first cabin was what is called "seasonal," which means you get to use it for the two weeks of summer in Minnesota, and then you drain the pipes, throw away all the food, and put out dryer sheets everywhere so the dead mice will smell better in the spring.

Well, last fall we tore down that little beehive. The bees actually swarmed the demolition team and got in their last licks. They are flying with the bats now (the bees, not the demolition team). Once the old place was knocked down and hauled away, construction could begin on our new place. And now I'm getting to the point of this story.

Wall Switches and Cabinet Knobs

We had chosen our builder about two years earlier. That was before the economy tanked and before everybody started asking me when I was going to retire. Both of these facts made me nervous, and so we delayed construction for over a year.

The firm we chose was Lands End. Remember, we're in Minnesota, so where the land ends ... the water begins. Nice. The firm is run by the Balmer brothers. Doesn't it just sound like you can trust them? I suppose in Chicago it would have to be the Luigi Brothers, or Sergio & Sons, but here in the land of sky-blue waters you want the Balmer Boys.

As soon as we chose them to do the work, we began to picture what our new place would be like. We visited several lake homes they had built. Some were mansions. No worries about college expenses here. Then we looked at tons of floor plans, mostly the servants' quarters for the monster places, but that would be the right size for us. Then, finally, we started to draft our floor plans. What a blast. What a pain.

For a while it looked like on our budget we could get a tiny kitchen, a not-so-great great room, a half-bath, and we would sleep in the car. We worked through all of that. And then I found out that the woman I've been married to for forty years had strong opinions on every cabinet knob, wood selection, stain colors, window size, and light switch placement in the house.

She and I could usually agree on things. It was her own conflicting opinions that drove her crazy and drove me to the office. Gradually, things came together and the plans were finalized. The plans were detailed and described what was called for in every room. We had a good picture of what our cabin would look like and feel like.

As we visited our cabin during construction, it was fun to see it take shape right before our eyes. There was always a copy of the plans tacked up on the wall. The project was completed on time and almost on budget, and we will probably never build anything again. I'm sitting in the new cabin as I write this, and it seems like I'm surrounded by a dream come true. We have also taken up residence again in debtors' prison.

The Bible says that God has plans for us— each one of us. He knit us together in our mother's womb, and before we were born every day of our lives was recorded in his book. Every moment was laid out before a single day had passed. I'm quoting the Bible (Psalm 139:13-16), I'm not making this up. Evidently God wants to get personal with each one of us. He handcrafts each one of us uniquely, throws the mold away, and stamps us MADE IN HIS IMAGE. Remember when MADE IN JAPAN or MADE IN CHINA meant cheap? Not anymore. MADE IN HIS IMAGE has always meant something was beyond value, exquisite, one of a kind. That kind of personal we like.

But some of us get a little nervous about God having *plans* for us. It's okay that God has good thoughts about us, wants us to talk to him, and wants to bless us. I feel the same way about my kids, but my kids don't want me planning their lives for them. Keep the blessings coming, Dad, but dial back on the suggestions. I can understand that. Each of us places high value on our independence and our freedom of choice. One of those is even biblical. Our American culture puts gasoline on this fire by insisting that we "go for it" or "just do it." So, thank you for the good start and the good news, God, but I'll take it from here. Puppets have strings attached, but not me.

Besides, it's seems like the ones who really do follow God's plans wind up on a mission field in Tanzania or in the ministry or having their mother-in-law move in. For crying out loud, what kind of freedom of choice is that? We think of God's plans as being like those plans for our cabin--every detail laid out, every outlet in its place, all the colors chosen. All the important decisions have been made, and you simply have to live it out.

So how can we know God's plans for us? How can we live them out without them feeling like a straitjacket? Do I even want to know what God has planned for me? Well, let's look at one guy in the Bible, and then we'll look at another guy sitting in his cabin. God had plans for both of them. Neither one of them had a chance, although each of them had lots of choice.

A Kid Named Samuel

Here's something easy to remember: Samuel's story is found in the book of Samuel. It's not always that easy. Job is found in Job, but Mordecai is found in Esther, Moses is found in the Pentateuch, and Gabriel is found everywhere. Samuel's story is a good one, primarily because God had good plans for him, but there's a little comedy and a little suspense as things unfold.

First there is Samuel's mother, Hannah. She was married to Elkanah, which wasn't all bad except he had another wife named Peninnah. Let's call him The Big E and we'll call the second wife Penny. Now Penny was able to have children but Hannah wasn't. Penny even made fun of Hannah. The Bible has a word for women who can't bear children: *barren.*

What kind of a word is that? Being barren was like a curse, and it was of course the woman's fault. In those days nobody ever seemed to question The Big E's sperm count. Yes, he had children with Penny, but that can happen when the little swimmers are slow or solitary. I know this for a fact. We had our daughter, Betsy, right on schedule (this is a chapter on plans). Then, when we were ready for a second baby, nothing happened. Nothing. What was wrong with Nancy? Well, she was barren of course, until I had a little surgery and along came our son, Luke.

So Hannah was barren and The Big E says, "You have me--isn't that better than having ten sons?" I'm not kidding (you can look it up in 1 Samuel 1). His wife is distraught and demoralized because she can't conceive, and all The Big E can say is "Don't worry, be happy, you've got *me.*" He wasn't the first dude in the Bible to need counseling, but clearly a little sensitivity training would have gone a long way.

> **God's plans for Samuel were not a steel-barred prison, but rather a divinely prepared path.**

On one particular occasion, Hannah goes to the Tabernacle to pray about her situation. She's in deep anguish and crying bitterly as she prays. In her prayer she makes this vow: "O Lord Almighty, if you will look down upon my sorrow and answer my prayer and give me a son, then I will give him back to you. He will be yours for his entire lifetime."

Eli the priest (The Other E) sees her crying and carrying on, and so he goes up to her and says, "Why do you come here drunk? Get rid of the wine!" How about the men in Hannah's life? Brilliant and tender-hearted all. So that counseling group has one more candidate.

Hannah tells The Other E that she is surely not drunk, but rather pouring out her heart to the Lord. "Please don't think I am a wicked woman! For I have been praying out of great anguish and sorrow."

So The Other E says, "Well, in that case, cheer up. May the God of Israel grant the request you have asked of him." That was a nice thing for him to say, and it did lift her spirits somewhat. So she went home and soon enough The Big E "knew" Hannah (that's Bible talk for they did it).[2] The Lord remembered her prayer, and in time she gave birth to a son, naming him Samuel. In Hebrew, Samuel means "heard by God." Hannah kept her promise as well, dedicating her son to the Lord. He first became the Lord's helper.

And then the Lord spoke directly to him in the middle of the night to tell him of his plans. Samuel listened. He continued to listen to the Lord for the rest of his life. He became the first prophet for the nation of Israel.

The rest of Samuel's story is in the Book, so I don't need to put it in this book. You might think that he didn't have an option, what with his mother praying, the priest giving his blessing, and

God answering her prayer. He was quickly dedicated, and it was a done deal, as they say.

But Samuel did have choices to make every step of the way. God's plans for him were not a steel-barred prison, but rather a divinely prepared path. When Samuel responded to the plan and walked the path, power and blessing came into his life. His name is listed in the New Testament's "Hall of Faith." So that's the way it was in Bible times. God revealed his plans, people responded, and favor fell on the people. Nice.

I believe that's still how God works. In fact I know it is....

In Search of Dr. Bill

I mentioned earlier (I hope you didn't skip that part) that I grew up in Bethlehem, the one with the stained-glass windows, not the one with the manger. Also, growing up, my dad owned a business—a painting business. His men could paint the inside or the outside of a house and hang the wallpaper. I think wallpaper is going the way of the shag rug. I worked for my dad for a while in the summers, and he told his men not to treat me like the boss's son. Evidently they were good listeners, because I got all the crappy jobs (if my editor says I can't use the word *crappy,* then you will see the word *crummy* here). I sanded the inside of closets before they were stained, or I got to clean the brushes with turpentine, which explains the loss of thousands of brain cells. For all of that, I made fifty cents an hour, and ever since I've had a keen interest in the minimum-wage laws. None of this fostered a desire to go into "the business."

Somewhere along the line I started thinking it would be nice to be a doctor. The idea of helping and healing people seemed good, plus the doctors I knew were intelligent, thoughtful, and could tell funny stories. In addition (and I hate to say this), they made good money, had a title, drove nice cars, and belonged to Golden Valley Country Club. Half of their wives were attractive, so I figured I had a 50-50 chance there too.

All of this took root in the part of my mind not being destroyed by turpentine. I wrote papers on being a physician, was an orderly in a local hospital, and drove ambulance for five years. There are a few stories to tell about driving ambulance, and if this book comes out shorter than the publisher wants, I'll just tack those stories on the end for padding.

I got good grades in high school, was a class officer, was on the #1-ranked wrestling team in the state, and dated a cheerleader (that would be Nancy, my wife). It seemed like I was on the right path to become Dr. Bohline (or Dr. Bill, if you lived next door). When it came time to choose a college, I simply said I was going to the University of Minnesota with 48,000 other Gophers, and then I would simply go to medical school there too. It's not that maroon and gold are my favorite colors, I just like to keep things simple, and that's why I used the word *simply* twice in the last sentence.

The first problem I encountered was that a lot of those 48,000 Gophers were pretty smart—real smart, actually. I thought all the real smart ones went to Yale or Harvard or tried to become politicians. Not only that, but some of these real smart ones wanted to be doctors too. I didn't think they had the right personalities or clothes, but they sure got good grades in those chemistry and physics classes. Which brings up the second problem. I didn't. I thought a lot of the pre-med courses were too hard, and besides, I didn't want to be a chemist or biologist, I just wanted to belong to Golden Valley Country Club. So I started taking psychology classes whenever I could, because I could get A's in psych, and I wound up majoring in psychology in an effort to keep my grade point average up. (I'm sure you already knew about my psych degree. It just oozes out in all that I write and say.)

Sooner or later you have to actually apply to get into medical school, and you have to take the MCAT—Medical College Asinine Test. When I sat down to take that test, I was flabbergasted that so much of it was not in English. I just didn't know what the questions were much less the answers. I started sweating when all these real smart Harvard types whipped through the test and turned them in early.

But I knew something they didn't. My application to med school would make theirs look like a bad credit application, and they would wind up going to veterinary school, not me. Why? Because I had references from the state Commissioner of Education *and* the Dean of the Medical School *and* Dr. A. W. Arthur. Plus handling bedpans as an orderly and delivering babies as an ambulance driver. Obviously I would make a fabulous golfer. I mean doctor.

And here's the kicker. With my grade point average (which I choose not to disclose at this time because some of my church members are likely to read this book) and the bombing of the MCAT, I knew this would not be a cakewalk. So my family decided to fast and pray for twenty-four hours. Well, that would put things over the top. You might not like my organic chemistry grades, but you can't argue with God and my references.

I waited for the news with confidence and a fair measure of denial. Then the news came. I must tell you that I haven't had a lot of bad news in my life. Our dog had died, and a cute girl told me once that I had big ears, but basically things had gone fairly smoothly. The letter denying me entrance to medical school was a different matter. It seemed surreal, heavy, and a little like I was reading someone else's mail. This couldn't be happening to me.

I had considered this possibility, but not in great detail, and I wasn't prepared for the kettle of emotions. Shock, sadness, anger, confusion, embarrassment. That's quite a menu, and each one seemed like the main course. Too much. Gradually the news got out. People shared their shock and encouragement and told me not to worry, so I added worry to the menu. It was like a door had slammed shut in my face, and it was the only door I had ever considered. Now what?

> *Our plans may lead to a bitter failure, but God's plans always lead to a better future.*

You're with me, aren't you? Haven't you had dreams and schemes that captured your time and fueled your imagination? Some say that's why they came to this country, to live out the American dream—prosperity, security, success. You almost certainly were asked, "What do you want to be/do when you grow up?" You began to plan and act accordingly. Some of us get well down that road, ignoring the bumps and a number of the road signs. We keep relying on our grit and determination. Or, worse yet, we keep living in denial.

And then we hit the dead end. No amount of determination can get us through that. It's a crummy feeling. Actually, it's several crummy feelings: loss, embarrassment, confusion, fear, sadness. We're really not sure which way to turn. But here's the thing: *Our plans may lead to a bitter failure, but God's plans always lead to a better future.* Always. Let me go back to my question at my dead end: Now what?

What about seminary? Now that was a ridiculous thought, but it had found its way onto page 117 of my mind. Back then I was operating with only about 134 pages, so this thought was way toward the back. Over time the thought worked its way up to about page 65, which moved it from the ridiculous section to the possible-but-not-likely section. As I mentioned, I had grown up in the church, my Sunday faith was still in pretty good shape even after four years at the university, pastors seemed like fairly normal people, and they had a title and could play on public golf courses. All reasons to consider seminary. However, pastors never really laughed enough, their clothes never fit very well, and they seemed ... well ... soft. Nice, but not that manly.

What to do.

Detour?

I decided to apply to seminary. I didn't feel "called," nor did I have a burning passion to be a preacher. But it was a next step, and I'm not one to stand still for long. The application process was straightforward, with no asinine test in a foreign language (that would come soon enough). They liked my psych degree, my references, and my mother. She had met any number of pastors as a church secretary, and the word was out that she was a lovely Southern girl with the gift of hospitality. I suppose "Give her son a chance to join the club" was one line of thought. I was accepted into Northwestern Lutheran Theological Seminary.

I might just as well have joined a mortuary. I realize that you don't join mortuaries, but I felt like I was in a segment of *Twilight Zone* called "The Land of the Living Dead." It was scary. Those first weeks of class were painful. Everybody at seminary seemed to be so serious and studious, even the woman at the reception desk. There was a hush all about the building, like a perpetual wake, and we were taking Church History and Greek and Systematic Theology. What the heck is that? Immediately I felt the same way about Greek as I had felt about geometry—this has no value in real life.

But the seminarians (almost a dirty word) were eating it up. I felt like a black pair of sox in white tennis shoes. Some things you just don't put together.

The only thing that saved me after the first quarter of seminary was that Nancy and I got married and honeymooned in Jamaica. We arrived without any luggage, which was fine by me, and the escape was heavenly. I'd had some experience playing bongo drums and considered staying on the beach and singing my sad version of "Yellow Bird." But we came back to Minnesota, back to seminary, and back to unreality. I immediately applied to medical school again.

Same results. Next came dental school. Then hospital administration. Those doors were shut tight too, so I kept going to seminary, partly because I'm stubborn, but I had invested so much time and money that I started thinking "Well, at least I'll get the degree." A master's degree would look good on a wall somewhere, someday, and not every bongo drummer had one.

Well, even people at a mortuary graduate after a while. So what did I do then? I took a year of graduate work! I thought I could be a pastoral counselor. I did some work in a counseling center and I came home every night and took two Excedrin. Listening to people and their problems gave me a huge headache. Scratch counseling off the career list. College plus six more years of schooling and no discernible job skills!

Nancy had been working as a nurse for those six years, putting me through seminary and graduate school. We had our first baby (see previous section on family planning). I was starting to think that perhaps I should get a job.

So I made myself "available for a call"--that's church talk for a job, a pastor-type job. I don't blame you for what you are thinking right now. *This guy is just a load. His wife carries him for six years and has a baby. Meanwhile, he can't get out of school and into the job market. She should have ditched this loser.* I forgive you, and you should have held those thoughts until you read the next paragraph.

I got a job. A nice little Lutheran church in south Minneapolis was looking for an associate pastor to work with youth and light candles. Bethany Evangelical Swedish Lutheran Church hired me and, when they found out I was half-Swedish, they loved me beyond all reason. It was easy to love them back, and they forgave me for my foibles and shortcomings, so I forgave them right back. It was fun working with the kids in the church, and five people said they liked my preaching (two of them were my parents). For a long time, when they called me "Pastor," I looked around to see if a real pastor was coming. They were gracious, kind, and generous—not with the salary, but with the banana bread and homemade pies. In the ministry you don't get rich, but it's easy to get fat. Everybody says, "Pastor, I made this for you, won't you have some?" What are you going to say—"I don't eat that crud"? When it's obvious that you do.

After three years at Bethany, the ministry became a good fit and had a good feel. Their love and affirmation blessed and changed me. They saw in me things I hadn't seen in myself. I wanted to be their pastor and give back to them. The seminary had been a head experience, whereas the actual ministry was 90 percent heart. My job became a call, a sense of having God's hand on my life.

Then came the invitation to start a brand-new congregation. That was thirty years ago. We called it Hosanna! with an exclamation point. I'm still in the ministry and I still think Greek has no value in real life.

Here's my point: God could see this all along. He was preparing me for this all along. God declares that he has good plans for us. This isn't just for a select few who wind up in the Bible or on a billboard. This is for you. Even before you were conceived, God loved the idea of *you,* so he told your father and mother to get busy.

His plan is for your life to be unique, fulfilling, enjoyable, meaningful, *and* a glory to him. That's a churchy way of saying he wants to be proud of you. His provision and protection are designed for you to live out his plan. Remember, he wants the best for you, and oftentimes he gives you hints and clues along the way.

Grandma's Wacky Idea

I forgot to mention something. Growing up, my family took a car trip each year at Easter down to Dewitt, Arkansas. My grandparents lived there. Mamaw and Granddad. Edith and Hugh for real. Since they had to put up with us kids for only a week, they really loaded up on the love. They paraded us around town, and people were interested in getting a good look at us because, for them, Minnesota was in a different country. We were pale faces speaking a different language. When I asked the kid next door if he wanted a can of pop, he kept asking me what was wrong with my dad. Finally I told him to get his own pop, and he told me he already had one. Dewitt was a real trip for us.

At night Mamaw would tuck us in bed, read Bible stories to us, and even sing songs. She sang better than Violet Larson (the mini-pope at Bethlehem), so we thought she was cool. Then she would kiss each of us good-night, and when she got to me she would say, "You're my little preacher boy." For crying out loud. Where would such a cool grandma get such a wacky idea as that? I just thought it was one more quirky thing about being in the South and I never gave it much thought. But I never forgot it, either.

Here's where I want you to lean in a little more. There's a promise in the Bible where God says, "For I know what plans I have for you. They are plans for good and not for disaster, to give you a future and a hope."[3] It sounds like he has some thoughts about how things should go for us. He really doesn't want to mess up our lives or send all of us off to Bolivia. In fact, he wants things to go well for us and doesn't want us to get discouraged.

Well, I like that promise and as I look back over my life, I can see that God has kept it. How about you? Have there been voices in your life that you can hear right now if you sit still? These would be people like a loving grandma, a dear friend, a special coach, or even a one-time acquaintance. They said something that touched you or seemed to speak into your life, not just into your ears. In the Bible these people were called prophets. Not all of them wore weird robes and had long beards, but they were, for a time, people whom God used to get through to others. I think he still operates that way. Are you thinking of anybody and seeing them in a little different light?

God can also use our circumstances to counsel or guide us. I kept banging on that door to medical school. Turns out I was banging on the wrong door. Every parent knows you don't give children everything they want, but you do give them what's best for them. Maybe God puts up roadblocks so we will try another road, one that's more suited for us and will get us to a better future. While our immediate feeling might be loss of hope, he's saying, "No, hope is over this way."

> **God seems to have wired me up to be more dependent than I think I should be.**

Were there times in your life when your direction changed or your course got corrected? I wonder if that wasn't God keeping his promise about good plans. I don't think God wants his hands on the steering wheel of our lives, but I do think there are many ways that he guides us to a preferred route.

One of my problems is that, too often, I just forget to ask. It's always been hard for me to ask for help or for directions. I'm kind of a do-it-yourselfer. That's fine when you are making toast or cutting your toenails, but I know that God wired me up to be more dependent than I think I should be. It's not a character flaw or some weakness. He wants me to depend on him and on others. That's how we are designed, and we are created in his image. The concept of "a self-made man" is a crock. That usually describes a selfish person who stepped on others and did whatever was necessary to get his own way.

God wants us to ask for his counsel, wisdom, direction, and blessing. He doesn't want to write our term paper for us. But to pass any class, you have to turn your paper in to the instructor for feedback, comments, and correction. I have found that God only wants to call me to my best. He doesn't want to flunk me. In fact, the only times that I have failed were when I forgot to turn in my work.

So I try to start each day with a simple prayer: *Lord, what do you have in mind for me today? It's Monday. Help me to look for you and to listen for you. May the path I travel today be pleasing to you.* Both of us like that prayer.

There's lots more to be said, but I'm going to let others tell you how they have heard from God or how he showed up in their lives. Turns out he is keeping his promises. For now I just want you to know (or at least think about) that God has good plans *for you.* He made you, and he actually does pretty good work. He likes you. I do too.

3

WINDING UP IN HOLLAND

Jeff Foxworthy is a funny guy. He's made a small fortune with his "You May Be a Redneck" jokes. For example, you may be a redneck if ...

- You think a woman who is "out of your league" bowls on a different night.
- You've ever made change in the offering plate.
- You think a hot tub is a stolen bathroom fixture.
- You think Taco Bell is the Mexican phone company.
- You refer to fifth grade as your senior year.

We have to move on. But you may be a redneck if you've ever raked leaves in your kitchen....

Okay, enough. This got me thinking about people I know and personality quirks I have observed. Do you know any control freaks? They want to be, even need to be, in control all the time. Most of them think they have this malady hidden from others. In other words, they think they *have it under control.*

I think they are easy to identify. You may be a control freak if...

- You arrange your sock drawer so that even if you have to dress in the dark, everything will still be color-coordinated.

- You agree that cleanliness is next to godliness—but punctuality is even closer.

- You don't like surprises, because you weren't on the planning committee, which you would have chaired.

- You start every week by making four TDLs (To-Do Lists): (1) Projects to complete at work; (2) People to call; (3) Errands or projects at home; (4) Things to pick up at Home Depot.

- You get upset when company doesn't leave when they are supposed to. Everybody has had a good time, it's "late," and the kitchen is still a mess. (My parents had a saying for this one: "Better to have them wonder why you left than why you didn't.") Plus, you know your wife won't be in an amorous mood for much longer.

- You think there should be two types of highways—one for you and a few other good, fast drivers, and one for the imbeciles who are just enjoying the ride.

I've come to realize that none of this is funny, because there are people who actually live like this. And another thing, I'm afraid my wife is going to write her own book some day and claim that every one of those examples is taken from *my* life. How could she? I guess I'll just have to...

I lost my train of thought because I had to go downstairs and floss. I do that every morning at

9:30, except when I'm in a staff meeting, although sometimes I step out.

In Charge of What?

You can get help if you are a control freak. I did, and now I even let Nancy have the remote when she wants it. It's a hard way to live, trying to control your life and everybody's around you.

And, do you know what? It's an illusion. We can actually control so very little. When we've traveled about as far down that road as we can go, we stand a good chance of learning some important lessons about relaxing, letting go, trusting others, and trusting God.

That's what happened in Katie Lafky's life. She's an energetic, high-achieving, hard-driving woman now in her fifties who came by her original "I can handle this!" attitude honestly. The goal of her girlhood family was to learn as much as you could in order to maintain control. "School was a hallowed place for us," she says. "We were all about wielding knowledge and feeling its power. What counted most in daily life was being right and proving the other person wrong. I learned early to use my mind and will to insulate myself, to protect myself from any and all setbacks."

For example: "I had to get my parents to quit smoking. I had to get A's in all my classes. I had to have the attention of the right boys. I could never appear foolish or vulnerable to someone else's will or words. This was how I proved I was superior, a cut above."

In such a value system, matters of the heart stayed secret. You certainly didn't show a sense of hurt. The intellect ruled. The family attended an upscale church in central Minneapolis that she recalls as "majestic, with beautiful wood and red carpet. I knew exactly how many squares were in the carving behind the choir, but little about whose house this was. God was regal, distant, and somewhat scary as well as judgmental."

It's little wonder that Katie pulled a double major in college—elementary education plus mathematics. She got married and taught middle school. In time she gave birth to a bright little guy named Mitchell, followed two years later by A.J. She was a woman in charge who was piling up achievements, one after another.

> *In Katie's value system, matters of the heart stayed secret. You certainly didn't show a sense of hurt. The intellect ruled.*

And then ...

In February of 1990, a third son, Max, was born—with an extra chromosome. Down syndrome. This hadn't been part of Katie's life plan. Here was a challenge that wouldn't yield to superior intellect. You could argue all you wanted, and it wouldn't even hear you. She felt blindsided, thrown into a whole different context that

51

would change everything about her future and her family's.

"When I told Mitch and A.J. that their little brother was probably going to learn a little differently than they did, their first question was remarkable: 'Does it hurt?' I stopped ... and took note that their concern was for Max, not how all this would affect them personally. From that day forward, they treated him as a brother to love and guide and protect—a wonderful example to all."

"Mashed"

It took almost a full two years before Max began to walk or put words together. Katie did her best to care for his needs, summoning her can-do spirit. Shortly after his second birthday, however, he got sick. The doctor ran blood tests and came back with a devastating report: leukemia, which is not unusual for kids with Down syndrome—their immune system is not as strong as that of other children.

"We landed on the fifth floor of Children's Hospital," Katie tells, "in a long, skinny room with no bathroom, our home for the next month. My little boy was hooked up to IVs delivering chemo plus 'mountain dew,' as the nurses called it—the only nutrition his body could absorb. He stopped eating, his hair fell out, and he stopped walking. He lived in his yellow Mickey Mouse jammies day after day. I watched anxiously and listened to the sound of his breathing as we slept side by side in a twin bed against the wall.

"God had me right where he wanted me at last. I was forced to admit that my mind and will were of no use in this situation. I could control nothing. I could give Max only what I was humble enough to receive from God. I needed his power and grace and hope, his arms to hold me up. Otherwise, I was going to crash."

Katie's spiritual crisis came one evening around ten-thirty just as a shift change was underway at the nurses' station outside the door. The theme song of a *M*A*S*H* rerun was playing on the nurses' TV. "God, I can't fix this," she finally admitted. "I just can't do it." And it seemed as if God replied, *Yes, I know. Just listen and let me do it for you instead.*

Looking back on that moment, Katie says, "I was helpless at last, and totally humbled. I became grateful in a new way for God and the salvation he had given us through his Son. I sensed God was right there with me in that little room. He would be my only hope for getting through the struggle of Max's leukemia—and beyond.

"God is so creative! In fact, he's clever. He knew how to claim me at last. He knew it would require a son with Down syndrome to teach me life lessons and lead me in the way I should go.

"Today, I still can't hear the soundtrack of *M*A*S*H* without being thrown instantly back to that crucial encounter with God."

Never a Dull Moment

Max did manage to beat leukemia. Daily life resumed, with all its complexities and surprises. One summer day when he was four, the family went to the Minnesota State Fair. "All of a sudden, he was missing! I ran down the street like a crazy woman, screaming for my child. My husband, the older boys, and I searched and searched for what seemed like forever … until suddenly, there he was, sitting in a chair eating an ice-cream cone! A couple was waiting alongside him. I ran up and swept my son into my arms, overcome with relief."

The couple explained that one of them had a sibling with Down syndrome, and so they knew that such kids tend to wander off. They had calmly taken care of Max until his family showed up.

"For days afterward," Katie remembers, "all he could say was, 'Mommy cry. Mommy cry.' I went out right away and bought him an ID bracelet."

In time, she took up a part-time job, at a Barnes & Noble bookstore. There a coworker told her about a new group that was starting at her church (ours) entitled "Uniquely Made" for those with disabilities and their families. Immediately Katie was intrigued.

Sitting in a circle with other parents just like herself, "there was no pretense," she recalls, "no pretending that life was wonderful. We could be honest and real with each other. And we could ask God to sustain us when we were out of steam, when we felt we couldn't handle one more problem." The distant God of Katie's childhood was now up close and personal, as near as her next breath.

Max's school life was a mixed situation; some teachers loved him and had the time of their life while he was in their class, while Katie says that others may have considered quitting the profession. By age thirteen Max was diagnosed with autism. "The combination of that with Down syndrome can make educators say things like 'oppositionally defiant' and other handy labels. It helped that I had been trained as a teacher and could navigate the jargon."

Max was in no way dangerous, but he did figure out how to "push people's buttons," says Katie. "I came home one time to find the babysitter cowering on the side of the sofa, while Max was holding a hacksaw he had found out in the garage and was just staring at her! I knew he would never actually attack her with it—but she thought she was about to be dismembered."

His twelfth-grade teacher had to clear the entire classroom one time after Max was found with a kitchen knife from the cooking lab.

Even so, he managed to finish high school and move on to the state-sponsored classes that run up to age twenty-one, focusing on transition to adulthood.

"Max is a retriever; he likes to hang on to his 'things,'" Katie says with a resigned grin. "His pockets are always full. Last week it was a giant urinal disk from a Porta-Potty—one of those 'hockey puck' things! Where he had gotten it I have no idea."

He holds no fear of strangers. His sense of food quantities is nonexistent. One time she caught him after downing ten cans of Coke and eighteen oatmeal cream pies. "I've learned to live 24/7 not knowing what's going to happen next," Katie says.

Lessons from a Special Son

Yet this mom is not beaten down with the life she lives. She laughs readily and keeps a busy schedule. In our church she has completed a number of training courses and led small groups on various subjects. She says that in fact she is a richer person for being Max's mother.

"I have learned so much from him—it's incredible. In fact, I'm still learning. Max sees no one's title. All he pays attention to is your heart, your intent. He has a keen sense of when anyone is being treated poorly.

"He wakes up each day with a heart ready to love and enjoy what is in front of him. He has less control over what happens in his life and who he'll get to spend time with than anyone I know. If my life were that controlled and scripted by someone else, I'd be a mess. But he has no worry. He personifies what it is to love as Jesus does. I am humbled daily by his graciousness—and he doesn't even realize he's being gracious."

> **Katie: "God was telling me that Max is his, and always has been. The Lord will take care of his own child, thank you very much!"**

Personally speaking, I have seen how kindness just spills out of him effortlessly. I was standing in the church atrium one Sunday showing off my new granddaughter when Max came by. Without missing a beat he commented, "Cute baby"—and kept right on walking. He had no need to hear a thank-you from me; he'd already delivered his compliment, and that was that.

One Sunday in 2010 we planned the service to highlight baptism and invited those who had never been baptized to come to the atrium fountain at the end. Max was among the 167 people who got in line that day. He knew exactly what he was doing as he knelt to receive the water on his forehead. Katie stood to the side watching, her face rapturous. It was a moment for the ages.

"God was telling me," she told me later, "that Max is his, and always has been. It's not up to me to control him or to organize the opportunities God has in mind. The Lord will take care of his own child, thank you very much!"

Along the way, Katie and her husband had divorced. After a number of years, Katie met Del in the "Uniquely Made" group. He too has a special-needs son, Adam, now in his early twenties, who was brain-injured at age eleven by a gunshot. The parents decided to marry.

"So now we're this hysterical blended family," Katie says with a laugh. "The four of us go out for dinner, and people across the restaurant think we must be a 'group home'! What a gift."

The couple does not know what will happen as the years keep mounting up toward retirement. It is quite possible that both Max and Adam may outlive their parents. Katie and Del are researching options, looking ahead to identify the kind of community their sons may need down the road. But they are not worried. It's like a metaphor Katie loves that appeared in a 1987 essay by a woman in similar shoes named Emily Perl Kingsley:

> When you're going to have a baby, it's like planning a fabulous vacation trip—to Italy. You buy a bunch of guide books and make your wonderful plans. The Colosseum. The Michelangelo "David." The gondolas in Venice. You may learn some handy phrases in Italian. It's all very exciting.

After several months of eager anticipation, the day finally arrives. You pack your bags, and off you go. Several hours later, the plane lands. The stewardess comes in and says, "Welcome to Holland."

"Holland?" you say. "What do you mean, Holland? I signed up for Italy! I'm supposed to be in Italy. All my life I've dreamed of going to Italy."

But there's been a change in the flight plan. They've landed in Holland, and there you must stay.

The important thing is that they haven't taken you to a horrible, disgusting, filthy place full of pestilence, famine, and disease. It's just a different place.

So you must go and buy new guide books. And you must learn a whole new language. And you will meet a whole new group of people you would never have met.

It's just a different place. It's slower-paced than Italy, less flashy than Italy. But after you've been there for a while and you catch your breath, you look around ... and you begin to notice that Holland has windmills ... Holland has tulips. Holland even has Rembrandts.

But everyone you know is busy coming and going from Italy ... and they're all bragging about what a wonderful time they had there. And for the rest of your life you will say, "Yes, that's where I was supposed to go. That's what I had planned."

And the pain of that will never, ever, ever, ever go away ... because the loss of that dream is a very significant loss.

But ... if you spend your life mourning the fact that you didn't get to Italy, you may never be free to enjoy the very special, very lovely things ... about Holland.

God does not deliver us all to Italy. Some of us wind up by surprise in Holland. And there we discover new things we never expected. We find out God speaks Dutch as well as Italian.

Katie was clearly headed for Italy—bags packed, smooth flight underway. She was in control. Then she wound up in Holland. She certainly didn't get what she wished for, but did she get all that she wanted? Maybe even more.

Most of us want to live life to the max. Instead, she got life with Max. Your first thought might be to feel sorry for her. But she's not asking for your sympathy. She would ask for your understanding and patience. She and Max deserve that. And both of them would ask, "Who's in control of *your* life?" That is a very important question.

Whose Bright Idea?

If you were traveling a road and the signs said, "Down Syndrome 2 miles" ... "Leukemia 5 miles"

... "Autism 7 miles" ... you'd do a U-turn so fast your Caribou smoothie would tip all over the front seat. You would not choose that route. Well, Katie didn't either. Who did?

God did. That's the answer most people would give. It's obvious, right? He's God, all-powerful, all-knowing, always in control. He's got his hands on the steering wheel of your life, so just enjoy the ride or endure the ride, whichever fits for you. Next question....

We all have people like that in our lives: Alice With The Answers, Eddie With The Explanations. As your wise uncle often said, "They are seldom right, but never in doubt."

Is there a point here? Yes, right on the end of your nose. It is this: God doesn't control everything. He could, but he doesn't. He surely does have desires and plans for us, but he didn't make me eat all of those little BBQ meatballs last night. And he knew before my 3:00 a.m. house-wide search that we didn't have any Tums in the house. But I don't blame him for that. (I blame Nancy.)

And another thing: When a little child dies, DO NOT, DO NOT go up to the parents and say, "Well, God must have needed another little angel up in heaven." That's asinine. God is a God of life, and his were the first tears shed. He is not pulling levers and switches to send some people to the hockey game and some to the hospital.

So then, who *is* in control? Wrong question, and it comes out of your need (and mine) to have things always make sense. We do want to understand and explain things and have answers. But as of this writing (call me if it's changed), that's unrealistic, unnecessary, out of reach, and was never promised to us.

> **God doesn't cause all circumstances, but we can turn to him in all circumstances.**

But isn't the Bible all about explaining everything to us and giving an answer for every situation and setback? No. The Bible is a love story, cover to cover, about God, who wants to be in full relationship with people, who redeems us from brokenness and sin, and who will ultimately completely restore all things, all people to himself. Amen.

I put the "Amen" there because that last paragraph reads like a little sermon. Perhaps I should have just made it a little Amen, like that. I do truly believe that God's plans will not be thwarted. The plans he made at the beginning of time will be fully, completely accomplished at the end of time.

Meanwhile, he is not a God who is in *control* as much as he is a God who is *constant*. Constant in grace, mercy, forgiveness, comfort, peace, and power. While he doesn't cause all circumstances, we can turn to him in all circumstances. "And we know that God causes everything to work together for the good of those who love God and are called according to his purpose for them."[4]

Translation: God didn't cause the mess or the mishap, but he can and does bring good out of it for those who love and trust him. There is a key to all of this and you saw it in Katie's story. The key is *confession.*

Katie's had nothing to do with her sins or her beliefs. Nevertheless (a fine word), her confession was heartfelt and transforming. It changed everything when she confessed, *"I just can't do it."* I suggest you memorize that one and live by it. It needs no explanation, applies to every living soul, and is music to God's ears. It's like opening the door for him and saying, "Come on in."

What You Get by Giving In

Several things are triggered by this confession. First, it puts your relationship with God in proper perspective. You are the creature and he is the Creator. In other words, you are fully recognizing that he's got more of everything than you—more wisdom, power, patience, angels, everything.

It also puts you in a position of full dependence on God. It's where you have always been, but now you are *confessing it,* owning it as the truth. And, as the Bible says, the truth will set you free.[5]

Now comes the good part. When you confess that you can't do it, that you're not in control, you have created an opening for him. He will take control. But not of your footsteps and finances. He takes control of your passions and desires by releasing his into you. All that he has becomes yours—the wisdom, the power, the patience. And you are able to accomplish things far greater than you ever imagined.

Three times in the book of Judges it says this about Samson: "the Spirit of the Lord powerfully took control."[6] Each time he destroyed many of his enemies or was able to set himself free from a dangerous situation. Romans 13:14 says, "But let the Lord Jesus Christ take control of you, and don't think of ways to indulge your evil desires." With Jesus in control, you can still choose what socks to wear, what car to drive, and what to get your mother-in-law for Christmas (get her a Sawzall and then borrow it), but you have ready access to the power and patience, wisdom and understanding, courage and compassion, forgiveness and fortitude that life requires. Especially in Holland.

My friend, Pastor Pat Moe, says everybody needs three things to be happy and fulfilled in life: (1) someone to love, (2) something to do, (3) something to look forward to. I like that. Unfortunately, many stay pretty shallow with that. They love Matt Damon, they're going to get their nails done, and they're looking forward to the next cruise. Or some variation of that.

Remember, many have dived into the shallow end and have received a spinal-cord injury that has paralyzed them for life. Similarly, if you continue to dive into the shallow end of that trilogy, you will inevitably become paralyzed spiritually, and you risk drowning in self-pity and resentment.

God's call is to a deeper love, a greater sacrifice, and a magnificent kingdom, here on earth and in heaven. Katie Lafky has discovered that while swimming in the deep end of life. That's where God often does his greatest work. You discover an intimacy with him you wouldn't trade for anything.

So next time you go swimming with a friend, point to the shallow end of the pool and say, "Now that's called Italy. The deep end is called Holland." Then explain everything to your friend.

Or just read this chapter to him or her.

And then, jump in the deep end.

4

LOST AND FOUND

I suspect most parents have a story or two to tell about the instant, overwhelming panic they felt when they discovered one of their kids was missing. It can happen at Macy's, the state fair, a family reunion, or in the church parking lot.

When our son, Luke, had to go shopping with his mom, he liked to hide in the clothes racks. The best hideaways were those circular racks with pants or dresses hanging all around, creating a neat little fort in the middle. Usually, when his name was called, a little face would pop out of the women's blouses, and it was on to the next department. Not so one afternoon.

Again, most parents could write this paragraph. First you call the name, then you yell, then you combine the yelling with running about, and you get the salespeople involved as well as other customers. The problem now is that every customer is a suspect. You want their help in the search, but you want to check their references first. Security gets called, and twenty-seven minutes later they produce an adorable tow-headed little boy who can't imagine what all the fuss is about.

You are so relieved and so upset you don't know whether to kiss him or spank him. So you hug him, extra hard. And you remember the first time you saw toddlers on some kind of kiddy leash. You considered it barbaric, but you're rethinking all of that when you find out the prices online aren't too bad.

Drama in Real Life

Surely there are no stories in the Bible about parents misplacing one of their kids. Well, you might take a peek at Luke 2, toward the end of the chapter. It seems Mary and Joseph—yes, *the* Mary and Joseph—traveled a whole day before they realized twelve-year-old Jesus wasn't in the minivan. I mean caravan. "I thought you had him." "I don't have him. I thought he was with you!"

Three days later (I'm not making this up) they found him back in Jerusalem at the Temple chatting with the religious teachers. Was he lost, or were they? Anyway, a happy ending.

There is more than one way to lose a child, and it doesn't just happen when they are toddlers. If you can get your kids raised into their twenties in fairly good shape, you generally feel pretty successful. The hard work of parenting is over, you assume. That's certainly how my dear friends John and Lois Carlson[*] felt by the time their

---

[*] See explanatory note on page 4.

married son, Ryan, reached twenty-nine and their daughter, Karen, was twenty-six.

Granted, it had been tough a few years before when Karen and her longtime boyfriend had conceived a child. He threatened to abandon her if she didn't get an abortion, and she nervously made an appointment. But that night, when she went to church, a total stranger came up to her during the worship time with an unusual question, what the Bible might call a word of knowledge: "You're pregnant, aren't you?" Karen broke down immediately.

"Would you like to talk?" the woman quietly asked. Through the counseling that followed in a side room, Karen changed her mind and canceled the abortion. She then promptly went the next morning to tell her parents.

"We hugged her and told her we honored her decision," Lois remembers. "And we said we'd do everything possible to help her raise this child." After Tiffany was born, Karen ended up buying a house just a block down the street. "She held a good job, paid off her car, and was in a Bible study with other single moms. She was so conscientious that if she ever went out to a movie at the mall, she'd leave the theater halfway through to call us and see how the baby was doing."

Then, in September 1997, a reunion of her high school class came along. While Grandpa and Grandma again babysat the now three-year-old little girl, Karen went to renew old acquaintances. A girlfriend from the past came up with a cheerful smile. "Hi! How are you doing? So good to see you again!" Soon she continued with, "Hey, let me introduce you to my friend Terrell."

The muscular young man greeted her warmly, and the three chatted for a while. When Karen picked up her daughter at the end of the evening, John and Lois sensed nothing abnormal. But they did find it odd to realize a day or two later that Terrell was now staying at Karen's place. How had this come about? What was their daughter thinking?

By the weekend, Karen showed up in a flashy Cadillac she had just bought, trading in her paid-up car. What in the world?! When questioned, she was evasive. And then ... they didn't see her around.

> *There is more than one way to lose a child, and it doesn't just happen when they are toddlers.*

Lois, now alarmed, called her at work, only to hear a co-worker say she had "taken a couple days off." The parents waited through another anxious night and then, still getting no phone calls returned, took a reserve set of keys and walked down the block to enter their daughter's house. All was quiet. On the kitchen table a note that sent chills up their spines:

Mom and Dad: I'm leaving Minneapolis. I don't know when I'll be back. I don't need family at this time.

Vanished

John and Lois stared at each other in astonishment. This was so unlike their daughter. They looked out the window; the Cadillac was gone. And most telling of all: Tiffany's car seat had been left behind! The Karen they knew had been almost neurotic about child safety, to the point that she would strap Tiffany in even if they were just driving to the end of the block. Now this?

The parents hugged each other in shock and grief. Fear gripped them by the throat. "Do you think there were drugs involved?" Lois whimpered. "She wouldn't do something crazy like this otherwise, would she?" John could only shake his head in bewilderment.

They called a pastor, who soon came to their side. He suggested they start going through trash in the house. It paid off; they found Terrell's full name on some papers, along with various phone numbers—and the name of a New Orleans hotel.

They called the personal phone numbers for two or three days, to no avail. Then they dialed the hotel. No, the desk clerk said, there was no guest registered under the name of Karen Carlson. As more questions flew, the answers became more vague.

"Have you seen a blond young woman with a curly-haired little girl about three?" they then asked.

"Well, now that you mention it ... yeah, I believe there was somebody like that around here."

They hung up the phone and stared at each other. This was totally bizarre. Within minutes they were back on the phone to a travel agent, lining up four last-minute tickets to New Orleans, for the two of them plus their son, Ryan, and his wife. The cost was astronomical, but they didn't care. They had to show up in person to rescue their precious daughter from whatever she had gotten into.

... Or whatever had gotten into her. Lois's heart began to pound as she remembered a provocative book that had come out in the late seventies called *The Minnesota Connection*. It told how scouts for prostitution rings especially liked to troll the Twin Cities and nearby areas for blue-eyed blond Scandinavian girls, cajoling them to come and "work." Their tactics included slipping a drug into the girl's drink, taking over her will as much as possible, and hustling her out of town, all the while beating her up and commanding her to do exactly as told—or else. Was that what had happened to Karen? Oh, God, please not....

(Weeks later, an acquaintance of the Carlsons', a pastor, got in touch with them to say he had just returned from performing a wedding in New Orleans. At the reception, he had overheard table talk about "the newest girl" who had just been brought into the business. The classmate at the reunion had indeed been paid $500 in cash to make the introduction, after which the beverage had been spiked.)

Face to Face

"We went from the airport straight to the hotel, arriving late at night," Lois tells. "There, in the parking lot, was the Cadillac! The next morning, I went down to the desk, got Terrell's room number, and then in fear and trembling knocked on the door."

Karen answered—and her face went blank with shock. Lois thought she looked high on something. Finally she spoke. "Just a minute, Mom," she said. "I'm going to get dressed, and then I'll come talk to you."

"Okay," the mother replied. "We're in Room 463. How about letting Tiffany come with me? She'd love to be with Grandma again."

"All right."

The little girl ran toward her grandmother's embrace. They headed away. And in time, Karen showed up in their room—with Terrell in tow, of course, to monitor every move.

"We spent the rest of the day together," Lois recounts. "The conversation was tense. We asked what she was doing these days. 'Working in a restaurant,' she said. But we knew better. You don't live in a hotel on restaurant wages.

"Don't you want to come home, sweetheart?" the mother pleaded. "We can help you get back on your feet."

"No, this is my new life. This is where I'm going to be. I know what I'm doing, Mom," she snapped. Her brother and sister-in-law could make no headway, either. By the time evening approached, Karen stood up to leave. It was time to return to her "job." The thought of Terrell babysitting little Tiffany each night made Lois's stomach crawl.

By the next day, the Carlsons realized there was nothing left to try. They fumbled around for some kind of parting words. At their last conversation, they got one small concession when Karen said, "I'm not going back to Minnesota—but will you take Tiffany? She shouldn't be here." The grandparents gladly said yes.

They flew home, the five of them, feeling horrible. But what else could they do? On the long flight north, Lois recalled an obscure Scripture she had discovered just a week before the ill-fated high school reunion, while attending a Cursillo (weekend retreat) at our church.

"But now this is what the LORD says:
'Do not weep any longer,
    for I will reward you,' says the LORD.
'Your children will come back to you
    from the distant land of the enemy.

There is hope for your future,' says the LORD. 'Your children will come again to their own land.'"[7]

At the time, she had been puzzled. *What an odd passage for God to impress upon me,* she had thought. Now, it was eerily relevant to her situation. She began to cling to this Scripture for a shred of hope.

That return, however, did not happen quickly, and there were more than a few false starts. Weeks of silence would pass into months; then suddenly the phone would ring at three in the morning. "Dad!" she would cry, "I need help! Get me out of here!" John Carlson would jump on a plane for New Orleans ... but by the time he arrived, his daughter had changed her mind.

Karen returned briefly for Christmas that year, but her soul had turned hard. When she got ready to leave again, she insisted on taking Tiffany with her. Lois and John sobbed as Terrell came to pick them up. They knew he was a pimp and a drug dealer, but there were no legal grounds to stop their daughter or retain the child, who lacked any evidence of bruises or malnutrition.

"We went to a lawyer after that, looking for recourses. He helped us put together a document to sue for legal custody of Tiffany. After it was all ready—and paid for—we sat down to read it one more time. And again, we started crying. It was of course filled with terrible accusations against our daughter in order to make the case to a judge ...

and we couldn't bring ourselves to say those things. Because we knew that the present person was not really *her*. We told the lawyer not to file it after all."

A woman who had been rescued out of the sexual trade called Lois not long afterward to say, "I heard about your situation, and I just want to affirm you. From my experience, whenever a girl's parents pushed through to take away her child, one of two things happened: Either she was so mad she overdosed on drugs, or her bosses killed her—probably because in her emotional state she couldn't 'work' as effectively anymore. It always ended very badly."

Who's to Blame?

Lois and John believe God kept them from pushing Karen over the edge. They simply went back to praying and asking as many others as they could to do the same.

"When a child goes off the rails," they say, "the first thing parents do is over-analyze. You try to find something or someone to blame—yourself, each other, anybody. It's very hard just to look at the reality and protect your relationship, to see what the real Enemy is up to."

The Carlsons kept making the mortgage payments on Karen's house for almost a year. Finally, they had to put it up for sale. A friend of theirs bought it for her niece to use.

One time when they had not heard from Karen in many weeks, they got a confirmation in the mailbox: a bill from a New Orleans hospital. They took it to a friend in the medical field, who translated the coding. As they feared, it represented treatment for sprains and contusions. But at least they knew she was alive.

There was no doubt that physical coercion was in play. Karen admitted that any attempt at leaving would be swiftly punished. Terrell's threat was "If you ever split, I'll have my 'homies' up in Minneapolis get your mom before you're even on the plane." This terrified her.

> *Weeks of silence would pass into months; then suddenly the phone would ring at three in the morning. "Dad!" she would cry, "I need help!"*

Lois, on the other hand, responded to her daughter, "Don't be afraid. God will take care of me somehow. When you're ready to get out of that mess, we'll help you do it."

Karen came home to visit ... and went back ... and came home again ... and went back—seven times in all over a two-year period. Terrell's control over her was indomitable. "She would come home, and start to get better in her mind—until he would call her. The minute she heard his voice, she would fall apart. And soon she was out the door."

One time she stayed home for a full two months. She even began a legitimate job. And then the phone rang. Terrell was here in Minnesota. He let it be known that he had a gun, and if she didn't come out to his car when he drove up, he would come see her in the workplace. That was all it took to collapse her will power.

Daily life, meanwhile, for John and Lois was agonizing. "I remember the second Easter so vividly," she says. "The church was opening up extra prayer rooms that Sunday, because there would be huge crowds, and John and I were scheduled to help pray with people. I didn't want to do it. *I have to go to church and see all these happy families, and I don't even know where my own daughter is,* I thought. *How am I ever going to survive this day?*

"In that moment, God dropped a single sentence into my mind. He seemed to say, *You take care of my children for me, and I'll take care of your children for you.*

"Something inside me rose up in that moment and said I could move ahead after all."

That day in the prayer room after one of the services, Lois watched a beautiful young woman with long blond hair walk in. She was very thin, and she held the hand of a little girl. The minute Lois made eye contact with her, the woman began to cry. "I'm in an abusive situation ... I have my little girl there ... I came to church for Easter, because I just *can't* go back. Can you help me?"

Lois and John put their arms around her and began to pray. When they finished, they placed a call to the local police, who came to escort her back to the man's apartment so she could reclaim her belongings.

Says Lois, "If I had stayed home that day feeling sorry for myself, we would never have met. We'd never have been able to help that poor soul out of the same crisis our own daughter was in."

They simply refused to give up. Lois prayed for God to lead Karen through dreams, to give her good memories of home. The Lord answered that prayer—but opposite of how Lois had requested. The phone rang one night at an unearthly hour, and Karen's husky whisper said, "Mom!"

"What? Karen—is that you?"

"It's so good to hear your voice," Karen whispered back.

"Where are you?"

"Well … I just need to come home. I had this terrible dream—that somebody broke into our room with a gun and was going to shoot me. Tiffany was sitting right here and was going to have to see the whole thing—it was awful! And then I woke up."

Karen did come home that time, but not yet to stay. She said that, in fact, the dream had come true for another young woman in New Orleans. The intruder didn't actually shoot her, but he beat her up badly.

Step of Faith

As August rolled around, the Carlsons went ahead by faith and enrolled their granddaughter, now five, in Hosanna's preschool program, even though she was 1,200 miles south. The teacher joined them in believing and placed a "Tiffany" name tag on the row of coat hooks for the incoming students. On Sundays, John and Lois would lead their prayer team by that coat rack and pray that each hook would be filled come September.

Soon thereafter, the night finally came when Karen, now pregnant, was in a restaurant bathroom throwing up when a woman walked in. She felt sorry for her and said, "Can I help you?"

"Yes," Karen replied between heaves. "Can you drive me to the airport?" She knew her parents had already pre-arranged a standing ticket to Dallas (not Minneapolis this time, so as to throw off Terrell's chasing). There she would be able to hide out for a couple of weeks with some longtime friends of the family. Within hours she was in the air and off to Texas. John and Lois finally welcomed her later to a joyous homecoming.

"We didn't push her for a lot of details," says her mother. "We just let her talk when she felt like it. Once when the conversation was flowing freely, I asked if she ever realized how far she had strayed from the things of God. Her answer: 'Every night, Mom, when I finally lay down to sleep, I feared I had gone too far to come back. How could

God ever forgive me? That was the last thing on my mind before I drifted off.'

"Well, the road back started with her knowing that at least *we* always loved her, and that we forgave her. Once she settled in here, we arranged wonderful Christian counseling for her. She went through Hosanna's 'Water of Life,' a weekly course that emphasizes overcoming spiritual obstacles in order to live abundantly. She came to believe that God had forgiven her, too."

Tiffany indeed started preschool with the rest of her class that fall. Around the holidays, Karen's pregnancy ended in a miscarriage. She went on to find a good job, and in time she even got the chance to buy her old house again. In the last phone conversation she had with Terrell, he made a startling admission: "I give up! I'm no match for your family and their God." His control had finally been broken.

All of this transpired, as indicated at the beginning, between the fall of 1997 and the fall of 1999. Karen now continues to walk in God's way more than a decade later. She works in the mortgage industry, and in her free time she helps many other women who need to break free of addiction and abuse. Tiffany is now a beautiful teenager who loves the Lord passionately and shares openly with her friends about Christ. She shows no ill effects of her early ordeal.

So, another happy ending. That's good ... but I suspect for some of you the happy ending is yet to come. There's still a lost child who is separated from you physically, caught in a life-stealing addiction, or living a lifestyle that brings you much heartache. Until the happy ending comes, you have to live on hope. My prayer is that John and Lois' story strengthens your hope.

Seven times Karen came home, only to go back. Her parents' hearts were broken, but they kept beating. By faith they enrolled Tiffany in the preschool program and had her name placed over a coat hook. By faith they kept a plane ticket ready for Karen to come home. By faith they remained hopeful. Faith is the channel through which hope comes. Fate makes us victims, but faith makes us victorious, in all circumstances.

Trust the Source of Light

Edith Edman, the godly wife of Wheaton College's long-serving president V. Raymond Edman, was credited with the saying "Never doubt in the dark what God has shown you in the light." The God we worship on Sunday doesn't take Monday off. If you tasted his goodness in his house, you can trust him to bring goodness to your house. Circumstances can be like storm clouds blocking out the sunlight, but God's presence and promises are backed by a rainbow. If this is the hour of darkness for you, trust the One who is the author of life and the source of light.

There's another story that some call the greatest story ever told. It's the Parable of the Lost

Son, or The Prodigal Son.[8] Jesus told it, about a man and his two sons. The younger boy wanted out of the father's household, but he demanded his inheritance before he left. He went to a distant land, squandered his wealth, and wound up feeding the pigs. "When he finally came to his senses" (one of the greatest lines in Scripture), he went home to ask for forgiveness and for a position as a hired man.

But while he was still quite a distance from home, the father saw his son coming. He ran out to meet him, hugged and kissed him, and threw a great homecoming party. Why? Because "this son of mine was dead and has now come back to life. He was lost, but now he is found."

There's a lot more to the story, but at its heart is what we are talking about—a parent who has "lost" a child, but has not lost faith. The father saw his son at a great distance. Surely he had been watching the horizon every single day, with a broken heart but with unbroken hope. And joy was unleashed when the lost son came home.

Can I offer a couple words of encouragement? In the stories we have considered, God never takes his eye off the children in question. While they may be out of our sight, they are never out of his. His rescue might not be immediate, but his resources are unlimited. He can still protect and prompt, guard and guide through events, feelings, memories, and even dreams.

Isn't it also true that the lost children in these stories knew the way home? They knew they still had a place there, and nothing could replace them. The return home was a little tentative, because they weren't sure what kind of reception they would get. But they found home to be a place of grace, healing, and reconciliation. It made the homecoming sweet.

Perhaps the most important thing I can say to you who wait for them is that you have not failed. Were you perfect? No. Do you have some regrets? Probably. Is that normal? Perfectly. The story is not finished yet and, even when it is, the letter grade on your parenting will be given by a Perfect Parent who knows your heart.

He also knows the cost of seeing a son set out on a perilous journey. That Son also returned ... and now sits at the Father's right hand. Do you know what they talk about? They talk about you and me and the time when we will all ultimately come home. What a party that will be.

5

CAROLYN'S GIFT

I cannot tell a lie—I'm the George Washington of Hosanna. I started the congregation in 1980, so I'm the founding father. My first title was Pastor-Developer, then Pastor, then, when I got some gray hair, Senior Pastor, and now I'm the Lead Pastor. I suspect that I will wind up being Pastor Emeritus someday. As you know, *emeritus* is a Latin word meaning "Whatever happened to that guy?"

Anyway, back then Lutheran congregations were started by a pastor-developer going out every day to knock on doors. Really. Cold calling, no contacts or references. Plus, I started knocking on doors on January 3, 1980, in Minnesota. So I'm talking *COLD CALLING.* My life was at risk for several reasons: frostbite, rabid dogs, ornery husbands, loneliness, and lonely housewives. Not to mention that I'm an introvert who always struggles in meeting new people. (This guy's a pastor?) I'm only telling you these things to spark or strengthen your faith in God. If a church can get started with someone like me out knocking on doors, there has to be a God.

Most doors were locked, nobody home. From time to time someone would invite me in, not because they had any interest in a new church, but because they felt sorry for me walking around out there in the cold. They would give me some hot chocolate and offer to call a shelter. There were times when I made some solid connections with people and my hopes soared ... only to have them dashed by the growling pit bull at the next house I would visit.

I first met Dave and Carolyn Kranz when I knocked on their door. It was June or July by then, and actually, they were out doing yard work, so I never got to the door. Dave had a hard time believing I was a priest or pastor or whatever. I had a polo shirt and shorts on, and I looked normal, not holy. They expressed interest in this new little church even though Dave was Catholic and Carolyn grew up Methodist, so they weren't sure what I was selling.

Well, they checked us out at the local elementary school gym. That's where we worshiped on Sunday mornings, and if you didn't like the service, you could shoot baskets afterwards. The Kranzes started out in the back rows, which made them fit right in because that's where most Lutherans hang out. They met some friendly people and thought I had "potential" as a preacher.

We got to know them better once they joined the Fun and Fellowship Committee. In a new church you want people to connect outside of the Sunday time, so this committee basically planned one party after another. My wife often chaired the committee; the Kranzes liked her and liked to party. (I'm not sure what class this would be in seminary, but my wife would be a great professor, and students would sign up several semesters in advance.) The Kranzes and Bohlines formed a friendship. We often had to have our own party to plan the big party for everybody else.

Nancy and I also started a couples' small group. Dave and Carolyn were charter members, and so we got to know a lot about each other early on. Dave is a teacher by profession, but he can create masterpieces with wood. He often gets inspired in the middle of the night and goes down to his woodshop to make gifts for people. Thoughts run deep for Dave, as does his loyalty.

We found Carolyn was intelligent, witty, organized, insightful, and Spirit-filled. She also had the uncanny ability to remember exactly what she was wearing at an event twenty or twenty-five years ago. Of course my thought was how could any of us know what she was wearing. So I started to describe what *I* was wearing at events in the past—but Carolyn would correct me, and pictures proved her right. For crying out loud. Also, her music ability and gifts brought her onto our staff at Hosanna in 1987.

There's so much more to the Kranz story, but you need to read it in their own words. On February 12-13, 2011, they spoke at our weekend services—just before Valentine's Day. I told the audiences they were about to hear a love story that would touch them deeply. Their story has had as great an impact as any story or sermon in all thirty-three years of our church.

Dave spoke first, primarily to introduce his wife:

A Husband's Introduction

Our story begins in 1970 when I walked into English 101 at North Hennepin Junior College and saw the girl of my dreams. Six months later I got up the guts to call her on the phone. I heard noise in the background and asked her about it. She was having a Valentine's party. I was totally clueless.

Three months passed before I asked her out, and another three months went by before I had the courage to kiss her. Despite dating two other guys at the time, she showed extreme patience. My dream girl became my reality.

We married in November of 1974 and are the proud parents of two sons—Doug, age 30, married to Sarah, and Dan, age 25. In 1980 we joined this little church of 180 people in Lakeville called Hosanna. Here our faith journey blossomed. When we joined, Carolyn said, "Don't expect me to get involved." She had no idea what God had in store for her.

She is an awesome pianist and God opened up an opportunity to play for the services. She is great with people. Then the choir director position opened. She is organized and attuned into music trends. Soon the Director of Celebration Arts position came into existence.

Between 1980 and 2003 as the music program grew, so did Carolyn's relationship with God. Her God-given talents exploded in glorious servanthood once she accepted the challenge of using them. How about you? Have you identified your talents and put them to use? If you think you don't have much to offer, consider this: In 1980 Carolyn was so self-conscious of her piano abilities she would not even play for my parents. The music at Hosanna that inspires us today is a result of leaders like Carolyn and a wealth of talented people who discovered their gifts and acted upon them.

Our most recent chapter in life started four years ago, when I got some news, followed by a comforting visit from the Holy Spirit. I would like to share this experience by reading a devotion I wrote shortly after this encounter. I call it "Miracle Cures."

Recently I arrived home from work to the news my wife Carolyn had been taken to the emergency room with major back pains. She was still there awaiting an MRI. One hour later the phone rang with news that challenged my sanity and her health. Carolyn's breast cancer from eight years ago had returned with a vengeance, virtually destroying two vertebrae as it wrapped itself around her spinal cord. Stage 4 breast cancer—it's a death sentence.

On the way to the hospital, my mind was a blurry whirlwind of "what-ifs." There was a storm brewing in there. Halfway to the hospital I decided to pray. The results were immediate. Faith kicked in. A tingling shiver leapt through my body. My knotted stomach relaxed, and the racing synapses of my brain slowed down from warp speed. At that moment I knew God would take care of us ... and we would overcome this cancer.

We were about to witness one of three types of miracle cures. The easiest to handle would be an outright purging of the cancer. It happens, and God can do this. Another cure resides in the miracle of medicine. New treatments make this type of miracle more common each day.

The hardest miracle cure to accept is life after death. This however may be the boldest miracle of the three. When Christ sacrificed himself, he promised heaven with all its beauty. Believing in him gives us hope in the midst of pain. Knowing that heaven awaits helps wipe out the why's, wilts the worry, and washes the "what ifs" out of our lives. Life is different now, but our faith is stronger. Each new day brings us closer to experiencing a miracle cure.

Several medical miracles have occurred since I wrote this. But there is one more miracle I've discovered since that day: *the miracle of time.* I never dreamed we would be giving this talk in 2011. These past four years have absolutely been the best times of our lives. I love my teaching job like never before, we have taken more time to vacation, we have spent more time with family and friends, and our love for each other is indescribably delicious.

You see, when you know time is limited, you appreciate each moment more. Here's the reality: Time is limited for everyone. Once you view it as miraculous gift from God, it becomes precious.

I have been blessed with the knowledge that God may call Carolyn home sometime in the near future. That may sound weird, but it *is* a blessing. I have already had four years of prep time to visualize and come to grips with maybe finishing my life on earth without her. I do think about this often....

I'd like to end by reading an excerpt from the popular fable *The Five People You Meet in Heaven.* The main character, Eddie, has died, and one of the people he talks to in heaven is his wife, who died many years before him. The conversation starts with Eddie speaking.

"You died too soon. You were forty-seven. You were the best person any of us knew, and you died and you lost everything. And I lost everything. I lost the only woman I ever loved."

She took his hand and said, "No, you didn't. I was right here. And you loved me anyway. Lost love is still love, Eddie. It takes a different form, that's all. You can't see their smile or bring them food or tousle their hair. But when those senses weaken, another heightens. Memory. Memory becomes your partner. You nurture it. You hold it. You dance with it. Life has to end. Love doesn't."

I am currently building memories so when the time comes for Carolyn to start a new life with Jesus, I will be prepared to carry our love with me until we meet again.

And now I proudly present God's valentine present to me—Carolyn Kranz.

Then Carolyn came up to the microphone. An anointing fell upon her and the entire room. Here's what she said:

A Life Abundant

I need to take you back to 1998-99, when I was first diagnosed and treated for breast cancer. There were three things I learned during that time. I refer to that period of my life as having "The Gift of Cancer." I opened that gift, and this is what I found:

1. The first part was to find that I *did* have the faith I thought I had. My faith had not been tested before, and I always wondered if it would be there when a test came. When I found I actually did have faith in God, I felt like the cowardly lion in *The Wizard of Oz,* crying, "I *do* have faith, I *do*, I *do!*"

2. The second part came to me during the middle of the night before my first chemo treatment in November 1998 when I could not sleep. I was afraid. All I could think of were the possible side effects of this treatment. I would be sick. I would lose my hair. I would get mouth sores.

   I opened my Bible, and it seemed that every verse my eyes fell upon had the word *trust* in it. I realized that the antidote to fear is *trust.* Do I trust God in all situations, or don't I? My answer is Yes, I do trust him. For me, where there is trust there is no fear.

3. The third thing I found in the gift of cancer twelve years ago was that it was important to allow people into my journey. This was certainly *not* my nature. My inclination is always to *do it myself. I can do this. I don't need lots of people encouraging me, loving*

me. But I did. And there were many, many people who loved me. I was directing the choir at Hosanna at the time, and there were about eighty choir members (well-known for being the largest small group at Hosanna!) who were the most loving people I've ever known.

It was hard to accept all that love. Was I worthy of it? What would I do with it? Then this realization hit me: *If I turn these people away ... if I do not accept their love ... it would be the same as turning God away.* After all, we are all he has on this earth to do his work. He gave us the Holy Spirit, and he gave us each other. If we don't do his work, who will? I had to believe that these loving people were being Jesus to me. By allowing people into my journey, I allowed God into my journey.

So those were the big takeaways from twelve years ago: *faith, trust,* and *people.*

Eight years went by. I became part of the world of "cancer survivors." I was thankful for my complete healing.

Then February 1, 2007, came. I had been experiencing severe discomfort in my back and left work early the day before. My boss called me on my cell phone that morning to see how I was doing. I talked to him while sitting on the stairs in our house. After the call ... I could not move.

Our younger son, Dan, was home. I yelled for him to help me, but his bedroom door was shut and he could not hear me. I finally called his cell phone from my cell phone. Off we went to the emergency room.

This is where things got exciting! I was in a curtained partition in the ER as they tried to get an IV into me to ease the pain. It's hard to get into my veins, so they called in the special team of IV people ... but they didn't come and they didn't come. I did not know how I was going to handle this pain in the meantime. Then it occurred to me:

I can pray! Duh! I visualized Jesus on the cross in excruciating pain. I asked God, who had taken the pain and sin of the world on his shoulders for me and for you, to take away my pain in Jesus' name. The pain left my body.

Knowing God was right there to answer my first prayer gave me courage to face whatever was going to come next. God and I were partners now. Eventually, the special IV person came and did her thing, and I was ready for the tests.

The tests showed a major tumor wrapped around my spine. It had damaged one of the vertebrae to the point of collapse, and that is why I was in such pain. And it is why I am now more than two inches shorter than I used to be! (I used to be the same height as David; now I have to look up to him!) The tests showed several other tumors up and down my spine and in my pelvis. So now we knew this breast cancer had metastasized, which automatically puts you in Stage 4 cancer. It is terminal.

Because I am the Queen of Denial, I didn't really buy into the "terminal" part very seriously. I did know, however, that this was going to be a fight for the rest of my life.

We called our older son, who now lives in Racine, Wisconsin, to tell him the news. His first question: "Why is it always *you*, Mom?"

My response: "Why *not* me? I can do this!" What would ever make me think that I am so special I'd be spared anything challenging? I figured this would become an opportunity for me to show what God can do in a scary situation. How would that happen?

I was in the hospital for a week. I asked Dave to bring my Bible. I'd been reading in Philippians. Now four words danced off the pages. It became clear that I needed to adopt them and live by them. These are my four phrases for life.

1. I will be joyful (4:4).
2. I will be thankful (4:6).
3. I will be prayerful (4:6).
4. I will be humble (2:3).

I shared those four things with my nurse; I shared them with all the people who visited; when I wrote thank-you notes, I asked people to please pray those four things for me. I promised myself that if there came a day when I found myself feeling sorry for myself, or fearful, or angry, that I would say those four phrases and see if they didn't turn me around: *I will be joyful; I will be thankful; I will be prayerful; I will be humble.*

They have never failed. I think that's a miracle: God led me to Philippians. I saw those words. I chose to adopt them as my own. They gave me life. They *give* me life.

§ § §

Was that the only miracle? Oh no. No way.

There's a certain kind of doctor called an oncology radiologist who studies your tumors and determines what radiation is best for your case. He brought me into his office during one visit to show me some very vivid pictures of my spine and its tumors. He called the major tumor "troublesome." We could not continue to radiate it, he said, without damaging the spinal cord and eventually paralyzing me.

Then he told me about a new machine just being installed, after an eighteen-month wait for it to come from Germany. They had researched all the machines of this type and settled on this one, called the Novalis. It would be able to radiate my tumor without affecting any tissue on its way. It would not affect my spinal cord—only the tumor itself. It was programmed to within one millimeter of accuracy to radiate *only* the area you wanted. Sign me up!

I was the very first person to have the Novalis used on the spine. Channel Four's Dennis Doda did a little segment on the Novalis, and they used me as the example. Methodist Hospital put me on the cover of their monthly pamphlet, highlighting the new machine. That machine is now used constantly for all types of tumors. The miracle for me is that it was installed and ready to go the week I needed it. I am a thankful person.

Then they told me I would need to wear a brace for three months. I will show it to you. *[Carolyn brought out her body brace at this point to show the audience.]* I now have abs of steel! Or plastic, or whatever this thing is made of. I wondered how I would ever wear this for three months. It affects what type of clothing I can wear. It makes it impossible to tuck a shirt in. It is a bit claustrophobic. It weighs four pounds. I sweat underneath it. I have to take it off every time I go to the bathroom, every time I change clothes. There's really nothing attractive about it.

But guess what? It is my best friend. It keeps the winter winds from reaching my body. It keeps the summer sun from reaching my body. Most importantly, it gives me the strength in my back that the cancer has taken away. I can sit at the piano in comfort. Playing the piano is my worship time and my prayer time.

Well, three months of wearing the brace has stretched into almost four years. What I thought would be impossible became something I live with daily.

How did that happen? First of all, I had to believe that God could do anything—even turn this monster of a contraption into a good thing. So I made a decision: I would *never* complain about this brace. Ever. What good would it do? And the truth pretty much is that I have never complained about this thing. It is good.

Chemotherapy started right away. To make a four-year-long story short, just let me say that I decided to enjoy my treatments. What was the alternative? Dread them? They came around all too often for that. So I decided I would dress up for my treatments and make them the highlight of my week.

My oncologist, Dr. Duane, is marvelous, as are all the staff at the cancer center. I have my favorite Nurse Nancy. We do a lot of chatting. She is interested in the lessons I am learning. At my treatment last month she asked me, "What were those four phrases again?" So I told her: *I will be joyful. I will be thankful. I will be humble. I will be prayerful.* She said, "Oh, yeah."

I am treated like a queen at my treatments. The treatments have been extremely tolerable. I hardly ever experience the sickness many people do. I do not experience mouth sores. I was able to work full time. Other than for treatments, I never took a sick day. How can I explain this? I can't. But God can. For me, it is a miracle. I am a thankful person.

It was the night after Easter last April when I had a heart attack. Well, this was a new adventure for me! I called the emergency 24-hour number. While I waited for a doctor to call me back, my discomfort was intensifying, and again I didn't know what to do. Duh! I could pray! This time I prayed by singing a verse and refrain of "How Great Thou Art." The pain left my body immediately. Again, God and I were partners.

When they put a stent in, they saw that I have a mass in my right atrium. It is a mysterious mass. Thinking it was a blood clot, they put me on a blood thinner for a few months. In August they checked to see that it had dissolved. Nope. Still there. Also in August we found that the cancer had spread to my liver.

So the heart surgeon, though he'd love to do open-heart surgery to remove this mass, said, "You have cancer in your liver. I wouldn't do the surgery." Now I realize I could die two different ways: From the cancer, or from a piece of this mass in my heart breaking away and killing me instantly.

In September Dr. Duane asked me what measures I was willing to go to to prolong my life. I told him I am not interested in any drastic measures. I am ready to go if we have used up all of our options. So I asked him why we're talking about this now. Do I have less than a year? He said, "Probably so."

I have had to ask myself many times since that talk with Dr. Duane, *Do you trust God or don't you?* Of course I do. That knowledge alone removes the fear. Am I sad that I will be leaving Dave and our two precious boys? I cry every time I think about it. Do I want my ninety-year-old mom to outlive her youngest child? Of course not. It's her biggest fear.

But will I allow God's light to fade and the darkness to overcome it while I wait for the end of my life? Absolutely not.

§ § §

Since last fall Dave and I have done some business. We've put our finances in order. We've had the legal papers drawn up for our will, health care directive, and power of attorney. We've talked about a memorial service and cremation. I quit working so I could simply enjoy my days and connect with people. All of a sudden, the only thing important to me is people and relationships. This is why:

As I contemplate Heaven, I'm pretty sure there's a lot of love there. Tons of it. Where does it come from? I believe we bring it with us. I believe we get to take all the love we have for others and that they have for us. And we get to meet up with the love that preceded us there. Love from the people who've gone before us. We reunite with all of that love.

> *Carolyn: "Will I allow God's light to fade and the darkness to overcome it while I wait for the end of my life? Absolutely not."*

I want to take a boatload of love with me. So it's important that I do a boatload of loving while I'm here.

See? Knowing that the end of my life is perhaps within the next year is a gift. I have been given the two-minute warning. I get to pull out all the stops. I get to love more. I get to prepare. I get to use my time with people rather than work.

When my friends want me to explain the peace I feel, I get to tell them. I tell them that I have the best antidote to fear—and it is trust in the Lord. I get to tell them that I made a promise to myself four years ago to live the words of Philippians: to be thankful and joyful and prayerful and humble.

When they want to know why God isn't answering their prayers for me for healing, I get to tell them that I believe God is absolutely answering their prayers. I am pain-free when I should be in pain. I have hardly any side effects from the chemo when I should be sick and tired. I truly enjoy having no hair. You might think it's the chemo that makes my hair look like this. Wrong. I keep shaving it because I like it this way! God has for surely answered prayers for healing.

And he has given me a husband who is so totally on the same page as I am with his faith. I don't have to drag him along and reassure him every day that I really am fine. He believes me when I tell him I'm doing well. I believe him when he tells me he is going to be able to cope when I am gone. He has never made me feel less than beautiful—through reconstructive surgery and, believe it or not, he likes me with no hair! He's always thinking of ways to make my weeks fun and enjoyable. We have the time and the desire to talk about all sorts of things.

And then there are my boys. I love them so much. We tell each other "I love you" several times a day. We have the opportunity now to make some terrific memories. It's fun, and our time together is rich.

At my treatment in December, Dr. Duane was making small talk and asking me how my Christmas preparations were going. I said they're all going fine, but I find it hard sometimes to reconcile in my mind that I won't be here for another Christmas. His immediate response was "Then *stay!*" He said they as doctors can only do their best to assess what is happening to the body physically. But he said they don't know anything about the spirit. He said, "Carolyn, you have such a huge and wonderful spirit. I believe that spirit is going to take you far."

So I live with such hope. I hope to hold a grandchild someday. And I live with a promise. We who believe that Jesus is our Lord and Savior are promised eternal life. Whether I live here and make more memories and see a grandchild and learn more and love more, or whether I die tomorrow, I have that wonderful promise. The promise of life after physical death gives me peace.

Either way I win. Every day on this planet is a gift. Every day brings me closer to the promise of a life forever in heaven. It is the same for every one of us.

My fear in telling all of this to you is that it would sound like it is so easy for me. That I have my act together. That I never had to wrestle with anything. But here's the deal: This is simply my story. The story of God working in me throughout my life. It is looking back at his faithfulness in the past fifty-eight years. Despite my humanness, despite the fact that I have been less than perfect, despite disease, God has loved me.

I was in my forties before I realized God loves me no matter what. I believe it is in accepting his love for you and finding yourself worthy of his love that you find peace in your life, no matter what the circumstances.

I guess that's what I want you to take away more than anything. God loves you. He knows you. He made you. There is nothing that can separate you from his love. Not life. Not death. Isn't that good? Isn't that the best? It makes me thankful. It makes me joyful. It certainly humbles me. And it causes me to pray with thanksgiving all the time. Thank you, God!

Singing on a Higher Plane

That was February. Six months later, on August 27, 2011, Carolyn died. She had played piano at a funeral service on August 3. We were amazed that she could do it, but immediately after that she began to lose her strength and her appetite. Dave called me on August 6 to say she wasn't doing well. I drove in from the lake to spend some time with the two of them. For days there was a steady stream of visitors to see the Kranzes.

On Saturday, August 13, Dave had many of our music leaders come to the house. For two and a half hours they sang to and with Carolyn. At one point she smiled and whispered to Dave, "This is my service, isn't it?" Dave told her it was. Later he called that afternoon a perfect foretaste of heaven for everyone there. That's where Carolyn is singing now. At her own service, we just continued to worship God and give thanks for Carolyn.

I believe all of Carolyn's prayers and ours were answered. She had precious time with her family and friends. She experienced little pain and a lot of God's presence. All of us saw her remain joyful, thankful, prayerful, and humble. She blessed and inspired all who came to care for her. She did a boatload of loving.

Not everyone dies from cancer. That's what the next chapter is about. But some people, even in dying, find a greater measure of life. A deeper portion. A stronger appreciation. An abiding hope and a lasting joy. Carolyn did, and we can all learn from her. Through her life and in her dying, she taught us to first believe and receive God's love and then to pass it on every chance you get. All of us are dying, so now is the time to apply that lesson.

I've always loved Romans 8:38-39—"And I am convinced that nothing can ever separate us from his love. Death can't, and life can't. The angels can't, and the demons can't. Our fears for today, our worries about tomorrow, and even the powers of hell can't keep God's love away. Whether we are high above the sky or in the deepest ocean, nothing in all creation will ever be able to separate us from the love of God that is revealed in Christ Jesus our Lord."

I suspect I'll never read those words again without thinking of Carolyn. She lived them.

Now, she's living them.

6

THE NONES

To be honest, I don't know too much about nuns. I grew up Lutheran and we had no nuns. None. You could be a deaconess, which meant you had to wear horn-rimmed glasses and keep your hair in a bun. I didn't actually know any, but I read about them in *The Lutheran* magazine, and there were pictures too. That's how I know about the bun.

My Catholic friends tell great stories about nuns. Just a word about these friends: Most of them go to Hosanna Lutheran Church, but they still want to be known as Catholics just in case their former priest was right about us Lutherans. In fact a few of them go to Mass on Saturday night and then come to Hosanna on Sunday morning. That way, all the bases are covered. I had lunch last week with Father Tom, the priest at our large Catholic parish nearby. He is a real regular guy. I just had to remember not to ask him about his wife and kids, but we talked about local leaders, sports, weather, and crazy parishioners. (His, not mine.)

I guess some of the nuns could be pretty tough characters. One Catholic friend (let's call him Tim) told me he still has a sore spot on the back of his head because of Sister Margaret. She was the math teacher, and in her class you were going to learn math or die trying. Fortunately, Tim was good at math. Unfortunately, Tim was and still is a rather free spirit, quick with a story and ready to laugh. So, when Tim did what was normal, Sister Margaret did what was necessary—a whack on the back of the head with a yardstick. Anyone who thought that was funny got the same. Sister Margaret is doing time in a local minimum-security facility. Also known as a seminary.

Another Catholic friend (let's call him Charlie) just didn't get in line fast enough. Sister Victoria ran the schoolyard like Quantico and when she rang the bell, the children were supposed to line up. Charlie had a little extra energy one day (every day) and when the bell rang and he didn't line up, Sergeant Victoria whacked him *with the bell.* The head wound required stitches. When Charlie got home looking for sympathy, his dad said, "You're lucky it wasn't me." Tough childhood.

It's interesting that both Timothy and Charles are quick to add that they deeply appreciate the nuns in their lives. Their dedication and commitment to the children were extraordinary, and when both of these guys needed extra time and attention, they got it. All in all, the nuns were faithful, humble servants. I just think the kids should have been issued helmets like any peewee hockey team.

Speaking of nuns, I should mention that Julie Andrews was in town last month. My son-in-law works in the executive services department at Target corporate office, so he had to escort/guard Julie Andrews for a couple of days. Now there's a nun! Anyone who can get a bunch of children to wear the drapes and sing in four-part harmony is truly a miracle worker. That's a nun any guy would like to marry. Of course, she married Captain Von Trapp and they became a solid Lutheran family.

On the Fast Track

There's another group of nones that includes some of your family members, friends, coworkers, and the people next door. The American Religious Identification Survey uses a multiple-choice form to ask people where they fit. I suppose it looks something like this:

Currently what is your religious preference? (check one)

_____ *Catholic*	_____ *Lutheran*
_____ *Presbyterian*	_____ *Methodist*
_____ *Baptist*	_____ *Smiley-faced Christian*
_____ *Pentecostal*	_____ *Channel 7*
_____ *Yoga*	_____ *None*

It's hard to admit this, but the Catholics usually come out in first place. Baptists and Pentecostals have had some nice growth spurts in the past, but not the Lutherans. Our idea of evangelism is to make babies and serve lutefisk.

Infertility and indigestion have put a huge crimp in this marketing plan. Plus, we're busy protecting our pure doctrine. What if Jesus had insisted on pure doctrine, even if it meant no disciples? Well, he would have been the first Lutheran, and Martin Luther would have stayed single and sober.

Here's the deal. When these surveys are given, they repeatedly show that the fastest growing category is that last one: *None.* In terms of religious preference the fastest growing group in America is The Nones, as in no thanks, not for me, never mind.

Who are the Nones? Slightly more men than women, somewhat younger, a little better educated, left of center. It doesn't mean they have a meth lab in the basement or that they don't vote. They can be very solid citizens who fit in a variety of other categories: atheist, agnostic, humanist, skeptic, secularist, free thinker, uncle, or boss.

> *In terms of religious preference the fastest growing group in America is The Nones, as in no thanks, not for me, never mind*.

They might have checked the church out and then simply checked out. They might have had some experience with certain church types and didn't want to be associated. Or, they've got the job, the house, and the flat-screen television, and they just don't see what all the fuss is about. They get some of their best sleep on Sunday morning. (Of course, that's true of many church attenders as well.)

On Her Own

So, let's talk about those heathens. Better yet, let me tell you a story about one of them. An atheist. You can already imagine how God feels about someone who says there is no God. Wait until you see what happens to her.

The Sunday-to-Monday connection broke down early for Kerrie Holschbach, whose family had been faithful church attenders when she was a girl. She and her older sister were in the pew with their parents most Sundays—until tragedy struck. An aunt of theirs was expecting a baby, as was Kerrie's mom; the two women were especially close. Both children were due within weeks of each other—and then calamity hit twice. Both deliveries resulted in stillbirths.

"I was still little at the time," Kerrie recalls, "but that was the end of the line for church. We stopped going, except for perfunctory appearances on Christmas and Easter. Later on, I asked my mom about it, and she said she was still mad at God. How could he do such terrible things to our family?"

By age 10, Kerrie's parents had split. The young girl's spunky spirit was already starting to show, so that she and her sister were placed to live with their father, who was better equipped to "handle" them, it was said. He was only partially successful. By seventh grade, Kerrie was trying out alcohol; by eighth grade, she was on toward marijuana. "One time while smoking pot in the park," she remembers, "I thought to myself, *Are we all just little pawns on God's game board? I don't think there even is a God at all.*"

If Dad ever did get the notion to force his daughters toward church more than on the two traditional holidays, Kerrie made her displeasure abundantly obvious. "I'd be really cranky. I'd pull on my grubbiest clothes in order to embarrass him." Confirmation class in ninth grade was required, but it certainly didn't "confirm" very much for Kerrie. She chewed tobacco during class and smoked pot in the church restroom. "I'm sure we were a very tough group for that pastor," she now admits.

The father never knew when his daughter became promiscuous, because she kept up her grades and managed to stay under the radar. She didn't mouth off to her dad—and in fact, he was distracted with his own dating life. He married one woman for a year, and then divorced her, marrying yet another one three years later. His daughters learned to live with ongoing turbulence.

However, Kerrie—ever the strong-minded one—made a remarkable decision by tenth grade to stop both the drinking and the pot. "The whole party thing wasn't so enchanting anymore. So I focused on schoolwork. I even graduated early, because I was tired of all those high school people."

As a college student, she completely denied the existence of God. Her philosophy professor at the University of Minnesota-Duluth reinforced her atheism. Kerrie was more interested in preparing for a career in social services, particularly helping those with mental illnesses. She would make her own way in the world.

An Old Friend

On a visit back to the Twin Cities, she went out with some friends, who reconnected her with Rodney, "a guy I'd known since first grade. We started dating. I'd drink with him a little, but not much. I don't like the way I get out of control when I drink, or the horrible feeling the next day."

Rodney, on the other hand, was naturally gregarious and enjoyed the party life. The two moved in together, and "I noticed after a while that he wouldn't show up after work at the time he had said. 'Oh, I was just out with the guys,' he would say. As for me, he called me 'straight and narrow.'"

Soon they decided to get married. But not in a church, Kerrie insisted. None of that religion talk would be allowed. "I went through the judge's script ahead of time to block out any references to God," she tells. "I was thorough. There was no God, and so we weren't going to pretend there was in the ceremony."

Rodney made good money in the insurance business, but Kerrie was never quite sure where it all went. Sometimes she would awaken in the wee hours of the morning only to realize he was still out. This led to arguments. "I didn't know where you were!" she would storm. "How could you do this to me?" Her husband would promise to behave better in the future, especially now that a baby was on the way.

A little boy arrived three days after their first anniversary. Two years later, his sister came along. But the chaotic life continued. On the couple's fifth anniversary, Rodney wasn't home—and didn't come home the entire night.

"That was when I finally got him to admit he was doing cocaine," Kerrie says sadly. "I immediately put my foot down. 'You have to go to rehab,' I insisted. He did, which took him away from us for three weeks—until he got kicked out for testing positive."

But soon, Rodney was back to his old habits. The financial tab for drugs kept escalating. Kerrie was doing daycare and any other job she could find to help make ends meet. She grew increasingly desperate, even consulting with a psychic at one point for guidance.

The couple was separated three times altogether, depending on the surges in drug abuse. At one point they foolishly decided to have a house built, thinking it might stabilize their marriage, since Kerrie had a good credit score. But before the first spade went into the ground, Rodney began using again, and the deal was cancelled.

"I had only one close friend to help me and pray for me," Kerrie says. "Mostly, I was busy working and taking care of the kids. I just kept my head down and concentrated on the next challenge, the next mess—like when he stopped at a car dealership one day and bought a new $30,000 SUV, paying for it with a bad check. I knew nothing until the car dealership called. There was also the time a 401(k) worth $10,000 needed attention when he left a job. He told me he reinvested it—but then later admitted that he spent the money instead. That got us into trouble with the IRS, which demanded a bunch of taxes. We had no choice but to seek a second mortgage."

Was there any light in the fog for this young woman? Not really. After yet another round of drug treatment, Rodney told his wife bluntly, "I'm always going to be an addict. You just need to accept that."

Looking for a Sign

Kerrie still had no intention of turning to God for help; he didn't exist. A woman named Robin, a fellow saleswoman of hers in the children's book home party business, would listen to her plight and say something occasionally about praying. Kerrie wasn't interested, although she did respect Robin, who was perhaps ten years older than she.

Finally one night in early 2001, feeling swamped by insoluble issues, she took a tentative leap. "All right, God, if you're real," she muttered, "then give me a sign. Show me something."

The very next day she got a bank letter stating that the second-mortgage proceeds ($6,000) that had been set aside for taxes had instead been withdrawn. Her husband had taken the money to Florida, she learned—to buy more drugs and resell them.

"I interpreted this as a sign that I really needed to get out of this mess. By now, divorce proceedings were underway, and in fact, I was seeing a guy who lived across the street. He wore a baseball cap that said, "I ♥ Jesus," but he wasn't exactly walking the talk. It was becoming obvious that I needed to find a different path altogether."

Not long afterward, she was in the bathroom blow-drying her hair when suddenly, out of nowhere, a reference popped into her mind: "1 Corinthians 5:9, 11." She remembered enough from confirmation class to know that 1 Corinthians was a book of the Bible, but she had no idea what it said. The impression remained strong, however. And where in the world had it come from? The only thing she knew to do was to call Robin and ask.

Her friend said, "Just a minute," went to get her Bible, and then read aloud these bold words: "When I wrote to you before, I told you not to associate with people who indulge in sexual sin...."

You are not to associate with anyone who claims to be a believer yet indulges in sexual sin, or is greedy, or worships idols, or is abusive, or is a drunkard, or cheats people. Don't even eat with such people."

To Kerrie, it was as if God was telling her in no uncertain terms: *Your present associations are up to no good. Get yourself a different set of contacts.* It wasn't long after this that Kerrie did the kind of thing she had sworn she'd never do: She walked into our church for a Thursday night service.

It was a small, more casual setting than Sunday morning, and she found it wasn't as offputting as she had feared. She kept coming back. One evening the leader spoke about Jesus' story of the prodigal son, dwelling especially on how the father *ran* to meet his son when he returned from the far country. Would there be a Father waiting to welcome Kerrie, in spite of her hostile attitude up to now? She wondered....

Summer turned to fall, and on the fateful morning of September 11, 2001, "I was home watching TV, like everyone else. When the second tower went down, I just fell apart. I was scared. What would happen to *me* if I died suddenly like those people had died? I didn't know what to do."

She reached for the phone to call Robin once again. "I'm just like ... I need to make a decision," she stammered. "What? How? Help me out here."

"Well," her friend replied in a gentle voice, "you just confess your sins and tell Jesus that you want to give him your life from now on."

"Okay … I think I'll do that."

She hung up the phone and dropped to her knees. She began to pray. She no longer tried to debate with this unseen God or put him to some kind of test. She surrendered her messed-up life to his fatherly care.

A New Life

It was a dramatic turning point. She couldn't wait to tell her kids what she had done. She even asked them to pray the same prayer she had prayed.

From that moment, we saw her at Hosanna every week, several times a week. She signed up for every class she could fit into her schedule. "My classic objections as a skeptic were washed away," she tells. "I heard solid defenses for the creation of the universe by an Intelligent Being—things that had never crossed my mind before. It had to be God! I wished someone had clued me in all those years before."

She started listening to the music on Christian radio whenever she was in her car. Some of the songs touched her so deeply that she felt chills. "I had no idea what was going on—I thought maybe the air conditioning was too strong!" she says with a laugh. "But it was the Holy Spirit moving in my heart, I finally realized."

Her divorce was final the next month, October, after seven miserable years. Rodney did not even show up for the final proceedings. Kerrie, with no child support payments coming in, began scrambling for a better job, eventually landing one in her field of care for the mentally ill. She sold the house to pay off accumulated debt and moved her children into a modest townhouse instead.

The strong-willed young woman who was once a militant atheist now puts just as much energy into doing God's work.

If you could meet Kerrie today, you would be amazed at her sense of balance as well as her passion for spiritual things. She is married again, to a wonderful husband she met online in 2005. The two of them have gone to Tanzania more than once on mission work teams from our church, even taking Kerrie's two children on one trip. Deeply touched by the needs there, they've raised thousands of dollars and organized a project to provide goats and chickens to poor families so they can better feed themselves. More than a dozen volunteers assist them in this effort. Kerrie and her husband have even put together a self-published book of photos from the outreach to help raise more funds.

The strong-willed young woman who was once a militant atheist now puts just as much energy into doing God's work. And the switch happened within a matter of months. "I was at such a low point, so broken," she says, "that I was grasping for anything. And all of a sudden—there God was! He was so real I could feel it.

"When I'm in a group and they start singing 'Amazing Grace,' I can't get through it without breaking up. The 'wretch' in the third line—that was me. How could God take me, who denied his very existence, and put me in charge of a ministry to bless many lives? Why would he even look at me, let alone trust me with an assignment?

"I don't understand. But I'm not going to question what happened. God has simply grabbed my heart, and I belong to him from now on out."

Persistent

I think God keeps looking after those who aren't looking up to him. It's like he can't help it. It's his nature to love people; in fact, it's his very essence. "God is love"[9] It's the first Bible verse that a lot of Sunday school children memorize. Learn three words and get a gold star. Nice.

But I'm wondering, if you are a None, what you are thinking of all of this. I really am grateful that you are reading this right now. I suspect you have lots of reasons not to do so. Good reasons, actually. I imagine that you gave the church a chance somewhere along the line. Maybe it was part of family life early on, or your grandma made you go when you stayed at her house. It didn't seem to hurt, and Grandma always gave you extra ice cream when your mother wasn't looking. Moms just don't let you eat ice cream for breakfast. Grandmas are cool that way.

Or maybe you went to a Bible camp once with a friend. You have a long list of memories from that week: cool counselor, lumpy bed, great hamburgers, weird songs that repeated over and over and over, huge mosquitoes, cute girls, hyperactive boys. At night around the campfire they told wild stories about Bible characters in a fiery furnace, walking on water, sitting in jail, eating grasshoppers, getting a bad haircut, or getting pregnant at 16. Some of it sounded like your extended family. The rest sounded like the next Disney movie.

Some of you (if you are still reading) have been hurt badly by the church or church people. You've been criticized or ridiculed or judged. You were made to feel like an outsider because you didn't know or believe certain things. Or something you did made certain people angry, and certainly it made God feel the same way, according to them. Or people whom you watched go to church on Sunday were absolutely no different from anybody else on Monday.

And now, someone who is "concerned for you" has given you this book and said you *should* read Chapter 7. Right there is one of the biggest problems the church has. It's not your problem, it's a problem within the church and has been for a long time. We in the church are really quick to tell everybody else what they *should* do or how they *should* act.

> **God keeps looking after those who aren't looking up to him. It's like he can't help it. It's his nature to love people.**

In the second book of the Bible (Exodus) God gives his people the Ten Commandments. You've probably heard of these. Stuff like don't steal, honor your dad and mom, don't kill any-body, and don't lie. These are pretty good guidelines that have stood the test of time and helped society live together with security and little bloodshed. Makes sense to most reasonable people. But what did the "church" do with these Ten Commandments? Early on they turned them into 613 *shoulds!* Amazing. Some would call this a miracle, but in reality it was a mess.

It's one of the big reasons Jesus came into the world—to straighten out the mess. When asked for help on prioritizing the 613, he simply said shoot for these two: (1) Love God, and (2) Love your neighbor (not just the guy next door, but other people in general. Although you could start with the guy next door). Jesus made it simple and said not to worry about the other 611 as long as we focus on 1 and 2.

Fine—but that's not where the church left it. We're back into the *should* business, telling people from our divine insight and knowledge that they should burn that book, they should give more money, they should not go to that movie, they should vote Republican, and they should know better. I think we're way past 613, and numbers 1 and 2 are stuck down in the middle. People should know this stuff.

What's Important to Jesus

That's what almost kept me out of the ministry. I felt like I didn't know enough—as if Christianity was a matter of knowing a lot of right things and whoever knew the most right things could be a bishop or a pope or have a rundown lounge named after him. I knew we Lutherans were right. I just didn't know what all was wrong with the Baptists or the Methodists. Every aptitude test I ever took said I should have been a CPA, where the numbers always add up and you can know that right answer.

I actually love the church. But when we insist on getting it right, we get it wrong. It's not about being right—it's about being loving. See #1 and #2 above. We need to take the air out of arrogance and put the hum back into humility and follow Jesus' example. The fact is, he drew huge crowds. Tons of people, lots of them sinners and nones. They weren't necessarily looking for God, but they sure did like Jesus. He did know a lot, but what he knew was totally grounded in love. People said he spoke with authority, and what they meant was "This guy sure knows what he's talking about."

They didn't feel judged or ridiculed when Jesus spoke. One time they brought a woman to him who had been caught in adultery.[10] I don't know who caught her or what they were up to, but she was clearly guilty. The crowd wanted to stone her because that's what the rules said they *should* do. Jesus didn't get ruffled or agitated; he simply suggested that whoever was without sin should throw the first stone. I love that part. He didn't judge the dumb crowd, but he essentially asked, "Who are you to judge her?" And they all walked.

He then turned to the woman and said, "Didn't even one of them condemn you?"

"No, Lord," she said.

And Jesus said, "Neither do I. Go and sin no more."

The only one there who could judge her didn't. I'm just trying to say that you may have been turned away by the church, but you will never be turned away by Jesus.

Maybe this sentence will be helpful to you: You may have gotten the clear message from the church that you need to *believe* certain things first, then you can *belong* to the church, and then you will *become* a better person. It's like you have to pass a test at the door before you can even get in. Then, if you hang around long enough, you'll become the kind of person who can go to heaven.

Meanwhile, don't ask too many questions and why don't you try out for the choir.

The crowds that followed Jesus couldn't have passed a test to save their necks. That was even true of his closest followers most of the time. But they liked hanging out with him. They felt a special connection with him, like they *belonged* there listening to him and eating with him. It didn't take long for them to realize that he was describing a better way of living and doing life together. He was inviting them, encouraging them, teaching them to *become* better people, and it stirred something deep within them. They saw things differently. They saw Jesus differently. They came to *believe* that he was Lord. And they invited others to come and see for themselves.

The churches that are making a difference today are following the pattern in that last paragraph. They are simply, genuinely inviting people in—into their homes, into their small groups, into their parties. They offer people a sense of welcome and a place to be themselves. No particular qualifications or knowledge needed. Within that relationship, faith can be shared or discussed, and new people can see firsthand if this faith has made a real difference. In other words, does what is confessed on Sunday have any connection with life on Monday?

I mentioned in an earlier chapter that several years ago, Nancy and I invited a group of people over to our house. These were friends or acquaintances from our church, and we thought it would be good to meet on a regular basis to talk about life and faith and marriage and parenting. We agreed to try it for a while and to be open and honest with each other. It didn't take long before we were calling ourselves the DaNile Group. Why? Because we came to realize that each one of us lived in denial. Not totally, not always. But when we felt nervous, threatened, dumb, or afraid, we were each pretty good at denying those feelings and saying all was well.

Did we need therapy? I suppose that's debatable. What we really needed was each other to build a little community, to build trust, to build confidence, and to build faith. We still call ourselves DaNile, but it is to remind us of the river we have sailed and will for the rest of our lives. First we belonged to the group; then we became different people; and, as a result, our faith has become deep and strong. We know what we believe and we know the One in whom we believe.

Making the Connection

Have I strayed a long way from Kerrie's story? Perhaps. She was once a None, an atheist, but the Lord still believed in her. He used a friend, a terrorist attack, and one particular Bible verse to get her attention and gain her affection.

Does this mean that God has a plan to get hold of every atheist? I don't know. But I do know that he has a desire to be known. Evidently, sometimes he "zaps" people, and other times he just plants seeds and waits. But at no time is he unavailable or unknowable.

There are places where you can check him out. Where you won't be judged or your questions won't sound stupid. We actually have a class called Skepsis at our church. It's for skeptics or anybody who is curious or coming back. We don't have all the right answers. We're just interested in the connection and the conversation.

I'm sad to say that we don't have any nuns at Hosanna. Occasionally I would have liked some to assist me with eighth-grade confirmation. But I'm glad to say we have a fair number of Nones. If they like hanging out with us, I think that's a good thing, and I also think Jesus is probably not too far away. Do I have any objections to that?

None.

7

WHO IS REALLY IN CONTROL?

I can't imagine going to jail, although I did go to seminary, and I have been to Las Vegas. Seminary and Las Vegas are both places that you have heard good things about and perhaps you have some relatives in each. You might want to visit one or the other, but having done that you don't want to go back. You just cross it off your bucket list, and in a convoluted way, you're glad you went but you don't want everybody to know about it.

But jail ... such a place fairly echoes with the word *loss* for me. Loss of freedom, loss of family, loss of dreams, loss of work, loss of reputation. As an introvert I like my solitary time, but only when I choose it. I don't need much space, but I love to look up at the stars. I get along well with most people, but most of them I don't want to live with. So, I can't imagine going to jail.

A lot of people do, though – and for all kinds of reasons. Most of our jails are full and we are building more. I'm not saying I have a better idea or system in mind, but to call them "correctional facilities" seems a stretch. It doesn't seem like much gets corrected. I do believe that some people belong there. Especially the ones who have hurt a lot of people.

One of our local stories is about a guy named Tom Petters. He ran a Ponzi scheme that wound up on the north side of $3 billion. (A Ponzi scheme is when you borrow money from your mother-in-law and you pay her back with the money you borrow from your brother-in- law. Pretty soon you run out of in-laws and the ones you can't pay back want you to go to jail.) Bernie Madoff is the king of the Ponzi schemers, but still, $3 billion is more than pizza money. Mr. Petters is going to be in jail for a while.

The thing is, going to jail really forces a person to take a long, hard look at the person in the mirror. What's it going to be? The same old bitter denial, or better discipline? Continue with the dead-end passive-aggressive attitude, or pursue personal growth, which begins the mental renewing and personal transformation? It would seem that for anyone, jail is a turning point.

Joseph—From Prisoner to Vice President

Most of us are never going to jail, but you don't have to read much of your Bible to know that a whole lot of God's people did. A partial list would include Joseph, Jeremiah, John the Baptist, Peter, and Paul. Holy Moses! (Actually Moses never went to prison, but he would have if the Egyptian police could have caught him after that "going postal" incident on the job site. Instead, Moses outran the cops and laid low for the next forty years.) Prison time is almost a badge of honor in the hall of faith. It's worth noting that every one of this list of people continued serving the Lord while they were serving time. In fact, for all of them it was their faith, not their failures, that got them in prison.

> **Joseph's brothers decided to sell him rather than kill him – options all siblings have considered at times.**

In the book of Genesis, Joseph's story is one of the most amazing. His initial problem was that, out of twelve sons, he was his father's favorite. Now there were only three of us in my family, but my younger brother was saddled with this burden. My older sister and I had to walk the hard ground of accountability and discipline. Our brother thought that curfew was what the Chinese said when they sneezed. After I paid my own way to the university, he got sent off to some fancy private college where he majored in none-of-your-business. (Notice, I was born in the middle and that's why I'm normal.)

Back to Joseph. He got a gorgeous Armani coat from his father and all of his brothers got to wear a garment called jealousy. Jealousy doesn't make for strong family bonding, so the first opportunity they got, they threw him in a pit. That was his first prison, but he wasn't there long. When a caravan of Ishmaelites came along (Ishmaelites were like professional wrestlers, but they weren't organized yet), the brothers decided to sell Joseph rather than kill him – options all siblings have considered at times. Off Joseph went with the wrestlers to Egypt. As soon as they arrived there, they sold him again to Potiphar.

Keep this thought in mind as the story unfolds. There is no prison or place where God cannot accomplish his will. What seems like a catastrophe to us might simply be the circumstance that allows God to reveal his plans and desires.

Potiphar's house wasn't exactly prison, but Joseph was a slave to Potiphar. And yet, Genesis 39:2 says, "The LORD was with Joseph, so he succeeded in everything he did as he served in the home of his Egyptian master." Even though Joseph had been abandoned by his brothers, that was the last thing the Lord was going to do. Because of the blessing that was on Joseph, even Potiphar began to prosper. So he put Joseph in charge of his entire household.

Things were going well until Mrs. Potiphar noticed that Joseph had a good body. I'm not making this up – it's right there in your Bible. She wanted Joseph to sleep with her, but he didn't want to be a gruesome twosome with the boss's wife, so he declined. Well, that didn't set well with Mrs. P, so the last time she offered the chance to dance, Joseph ran out of the house. The problem was that his shirt had come off in her hot little hands, and when he ran off, she started screaming, "Rape!" Guess where Joseph's next stop was?

Here's another thing to remember – we see it all the time in the Bible. God's plans cannot be thwarted by false accusations or evil plots. Again and again, he takes what others have meant for evil or harm and turns it into occasions to reveal his glory and his sovereign rule. I like that about God. And, if that's not enough, we see that God often chooses to bless an entire nation through one courageous servant.

So the Lord was still with Joseph.[11] The warden put him in charge of everything and had no more worries. This time he was in for over two years, but he got a chance to use one of his special God-given gifts: He could interpret dreams. He helped some of his inmates understand what their dreams or visions meant. For some it was good; for some it wasn't. No matter what, Joseph always gave God the credit for his special gift.

In time Pharaoh (Potiphar's boss) had a dream that nobody could understand. Joseph's former cellmate remembered Joseph's gift and mentioned it to Pharaoh. When asked to interpret the dream, Joseph assured Pharaoh that he had no power to do it, "but God can tell you what it means and set you at ease."[12] Quite simply the dream meant there were seven good years coming for Egypt, followed by seven years of famine. Pharaoh accepted this as the truth, so he put Joseph in charge of a nationwide program to stockpile during the good years so they could survive the famine. Joseph was literally the number two man in the land. He went from victim and prisoner to vice president at age 30.

God remains faithful to those who place their faith in him. He neither abandons nor neglects his loyal followers. That's a great message. And it became a pretty good musical. A few years back, when *Joseph and the Amazing Technicolor Dreamcoat* came to town, Nancy and I went to see it. Donny Osmond played Joseph. Ahhh, Donny in a loincloth. It was a fantastic Broadway production with costumes and choreography that rocked the house. Pharaoh was played by an Elvis impersonator, and Joseph's brothers were a singing, dancing chorus that would easily win on *Dancing with the Stars*.

See, that's what we often do with Bible stories. We read them to kids, or we turn them into fantasy. It's all very entertaining, but on Monday morning you have to go to work and leave the fantasy and visions of Donny behind.

Modern-day Joseph

Until you meet a modern-day Joseph. His name is Chris. He tells his story to others whenever he can because he feels that's the best way to give credit to God, who rescued him. But I'm getting ahead...

I would describe Chris' upbringing except you've already seen it – perhaps a thousand times. House in the suburbs, mom and dad, one brother, no dysfunction, no divorce, no abuse. They even went to church, although Chris would tell you that while he went, he wasn't there. He believed, but he didn't participate. "I was still in control." We'll get back to that thought later.

You'd like Chris the second you met him. Everybody does. He's friendly, gregarious (sometimes authors are just determined to use a particular word), funny, and he loves to help people. I know God smiled after he approved the design plan for Chris. Did I mention that Chris liked to party when he was growing up? Those parties became the gateway to alcohol and the occasional use of drugs. Some people can do that and still remain in control. Others can't.

The occasional use quickly became every weekend. Soon it was every day. That changed everything. It's like there was a new boss in Chris' life, and this one was a tyrant. A concoction of alcohol, weed, and cocaine would carry him from one day to the next, but methamphetamine brought him down. He couldn't go one day without it. And so Chris started to sell drugs in order to feed his own addiction.

None of this put Chris in the gutter or some shelter for the homeless. Somehow he managed to keep going to work and coming home after work. He didn't always come straight home and he was often lucky to get there, but the deceptions and lies were forming a trap from which he would not escape.

The delusions made him think he would never get caught. Each day he battled to hide it from his wife and family. He even tried treatment, but it just made him a better addict, "controlling" his own addiction. That's what he thought ... until one Wednesday night he came walking out of our church, and in the parking lot federal agents arrested him. Chris went from church to a jail cell in a matter of hours.

Chris would later say, "I felt scared, despair, disbelief. This was Hennepin County Jail—the real deal. I was in a drunk tank and coming down off of meth. People were fighting. It was crazy. What had I gotten myself into?"

It became clear early on that the authorities had all they needed to convict Chris on possession and sales. He was facing a ten-year sentence in federal prison. The fog of delusion was lifted and the option of denial was removed. Like standing almost naked in the glaring sunlight, everything Chris was and had done was in full view. As a husband, dad, son, and friend, he had failed everyone who loved him.

The shame and guilt were crushing. He couldn't imagine, couldn't fathom, how anyone would ever forgive him. He had heard plenty about forgiveness, but he had never personally experienced it. Now he was in position to listen, learn, understand, and grasp that kind of love. It became his lifeline.

The New High

Chris was put on pretrial probation. He could be out of jail until his trial, but he had to submit to drug tests. His wife, his parents, and one of our pastors started to draw closer to him. Many prayers were spoken and many Scripture promises recited. A hope began to stir within Chris. But there still was a power over him that needed to be broken. He flunked a drug test just two weeks later. Prison would be his home for some time to come.

"I was drunk and a bit relieved that I was finally beaten. I was tired. This was the lowest of the lows. I was put in solitary, and that was peaceful for me. I began to pray by myself. I was open to the possibility that Jesus had even died for someone like me, but I didn't know how long I would be in prison. That made me worry."

Chris describes his "aha" moment. "I was reading my Bible and praying, when I guess a light bulb went on. I just kept thinking LET GO AND LET GOD. LET GO AND LET GOD. Could it be that easy? I suddenly believed it was. My Bible now wasn't just words on the page. It was as if God was speaking to me and telling me how to live my life. It filled me to overflowing."

While waiting to be sentenced, Chris *turned his life over to God.* That's how he puts it. Those six words look so simple. I want to dress them up and write a few paragraphs about lights, angels, visions, and Chris listening to all my sermons. It seems like there should be more drama and a drum roll, not just a prison cell and a Bible. This was a real-life rescue operation like those

> *Chris's desire totally shifted from being in control to being in Christ.*

Chilean miners being brought up out of that dark, deadly shaft a few years ago. I just think that Chris' story is equally compelling.

Chris' surrender was all God needed to begin reshaping the man he had always wanted Chris to be. He couldn't get enough of his Bible. His desire totally shifted from being in control to being in Christ. This led to deeper conversations with his wife. He began to understand how she might be able to forgive him and keep loving him.

"We talked about everything. For the first time in a long time I told her the truth – every lie was exposed. I felt clean. *Clean.* Our conversations were constructive, not destructive. We were building each other up, not destroying each other. We talked about God, and we prayed for his will."

Hope became the new "high" for Chris. It's like his heart started to beat again, so that relationships blossomed. But he was still in jail. Many of us wrote letters on his behalf. Prayer chains were busy. The hope was that Chris would receive only probation or some kind of suspended sentence. But the judge had other plans, and finally the sentence was handed down: forty-two months. Three and a half years. Once again the reality of what Chris had done and the demand that justice be served came crashing in.

Something was different this time, however. The flame of faith that the Lord had ignited would not be extinguished. Chris will actually tell you that this is where his life started to get better.

God's Real Work

Chris started to look for and clearly see God's hand upon him. His time would be served at a minimum-security facility in Yankton, South Dakota. He settled into a routine where meals and mail call were the biggest parts of his day. He got a job mowing grass in the summer and shoveling snow in the winter. Pay started at 3 cents per hour and you could work your way up to 12 cents per hour. Within this routine God was doing his real work of recovery and reconciliation.

Chris read his Bible every day, went to church every Sunday and Wednesday, and loved inmate Bible study, which they called "The Upper Room." Two local churches came in to do the worship services, and there was a prison band that could really make a joyful noise. Chris was full-immersion baptized and was encouraged to speak in tongues. The tongues didn't happen but the tears flowed as he felt the Holy Spirit fill him up.

He wrote to his wife, Jenni, every day and called three times a week. His whole family could visit every three months. Finally he could hold and hug his two kids again—something he hadn't done for three months. He and Jenni prayed together and counted their blessings. One of the "miracles" they experienced related to their finances. Chris had nearly bankrupted the family, but month by month God provided just enough for the bills to be paid. There was some income from Jenni's work, some from gifts, and the rest just couldn't be explained.

Through a community work release program Chris was able to work outside the prison at Habitat for Humanity, the Boy Scouts, a local museum and a theater. He was paid with lunch at a fast-food restaurant of his choice. Chris saw that as yet another blessing. I suppose you could debate that. He and Jenni attended a marriage course and a parenting course together.

Another huge break came when Chris was accepted into a 500-hour inpatient drug treatment program that would cut one year off his sentence when completed. And, Chris found out his case worker was a Christian. As Chris says, "He was the man in charge of my life while I was in prison, and God was in charge of his."

After two years of time served, Chris was released to a VOA halfway house, where he would complete the last six months of his sentence. Weekend passes got him home, and a real job became part of his life once again. Today, Chris is an employee at Hosanna, the very church where he was arrested. He is in charge of all of our computers and is brilliant at what he does. He also consults with many other churches and small businesses. He and Jenni have a huge heart for our prison ministries. They constantly visit inmates, write letters, and send Bibles and other Christian books to encourage them.

Chris may write a book someday. If he does, I know this line will be in it: "Everything the Devil tried to use for his purposes, God used for his own glory. Everything the Devil stole from me, God has returned seven times." He would also want you to know that his favorite verses are Romans 8:5-6, "Those who are dominated by the sinful nature think about sinful things, but those who are *controlled by the Holy Spirit* think about things that please the Spirit. So letting your sinful nature control your mind leads to death. But *letting the Spirit control your mind leads to life and peace.*" That's not just a Bible passage for Chris or a Sunday preaching text. That's his daily reality, seven days a week.

Another Verdict

Most of us will never wind up going to jail, but there are many ways we get locked up. Prison cells can have names like *anger, abuse, shame, addiction, pride,* or just simply *lost.* We are just as trapped in these cells as any that have bars. And the sense of loss is just as great. We lose direction, time, hope, and intimacy. Freedom is a foreign word. Relationships are diminished or destroyed, and joy dies out like a birthday candle. For some people, all of this can seem like a life sentence.

But there is another verdict that has been handed down. Jesus said it: "You will know the truth, and the truth will set you *free.*"[13] Jesus came to tell us the truth about God's grace, mercy, and forgiveness. His death on the cross revealed that there simply are *no limits* to God's love. I suppose there is truth that can be written in a book without changing a thing—for example, 2+2=4. That's the truth, but it will never mend a broken heart or restore a relationship.

God designed you by hand, you are created in his image, he has good plans for you, and he wants you to live for all eternity with him and other believers. That's the truth. But it will never be personal or powerful *until you put him in control.* Some people think that's another kind of prison; they want to remain in control. Let me kindly ask, "How's that working for you?" Remember to set aside delusion and denial and be honest with yourself. I don't mean to get in your face, I just know that the Lord has something better for you.

Maybe this will help. Whenever I fly some-where, I'm perfectly content to sit in seat 14A (by the window). I don't know how to fly a jet plane, and so you wouldn't want me in the pilot's seat. I don't want to be there either. I'm better off trusting my life to someone who knows how to get me where I want to go. Somehow we've gotten the idea that living a life with a trillion options, issues, emotions, ideas, and intricacies is easier than flying a jet plane. Anyone can do it and should be in control. Are you really surprised that there are so many crashes and disasters?

God wants you to be free. He does identify some boundaries for how you live your life, but within those boundaries there is joy, peace, intimacy, harmony, purpose, direction, and eternity. And there is freedom. Chris says it well: "God doesn't put us in prison. He gets us out." I fully agree.

8

ASK AND EXPECT

Nothing quite gets your attention like bad news from the doctor. Mary Nelson was a trim, busy 47-year-old suburban wife and mother of two when she got the shock of her life one August day: invasive breast cancer. "I'd had no history of cancer in my family," she says. "My life was under control. I'd even had a negative mammogram recently! Cancer was something that happened to other people, certainly not me."

The doctors initially thought it was a very small tumor that could be removed surgically, and that would be the end of it. But in the operating room, they found the cancer had spread into two of Mary's lymph nodes. That called for eight rounds of chemotherapy, six weeks of radiation—and a year of being bald.

This clearly did not mesh with the personality of a high-achieving perfectionist ("At the age of four, I had colored every page in my Cinderella coloring book *in order* and *never* colored outside the lines"). She had gone on to earn two college degrees, teach dental students at the University of Minnesota, then gone back for an MBA and opened up her own healthcare communications consulting firm. Writing articles for publication or standing up in front of seminar audiences was common for her.

The same *über*-confidence had carried over into church life. "I was there every week, of course," she says, "with a huge spirit of pride that God needed to break. He had my head—but not yet my heart. He was the Lord of Sunday morning, and that was it."

When I or one of the other pastors would encourage the Hosanna people to bring their Bibles to church, Mary would sit there thinking to herself, *Why? What's the point? I already know what it says.* When at the end of the service we'd suggest that individual prayer was available in the chapel, Mary would think, *They want me to open up my personal space to somebody I don't even know? No, thanks.*

But now ... everything was different. She began reaching out for support wherever she could find it, starting in the prayer chapel. "When people laid their hands on me and prayed over me, I felt for the first time the *presence* of God," she says. "When they wiped tears from my eyes, it was as if God was doing those things himself.

"People would call me, send me cards, and the community of believers was beyond anything I'd ever imagined. Other friends of mine almost seemed to be backing away from me because they felt awkward around somebody with cancer. These people, on the other hand, drew in closer."

Mary's two children at this point were both seniors: her son in college, her daughter in high school. While her daughter was away on a school dance team trip to Disney World, Mary went ahead and had her husband, Howie, shave off the rest of her rapidly thinning hair. "I'll never forget the day I picked her up at the airport," she says. "She took one look at my new wig and had a major meltdown. 'I can't look at you!' she exploded. As soon as we got home, she went into her bedroom and slammed the door.

"Her dad then went in and had a quiet talk with her, after which she stabilized. His approach to my cancer was very calming. He treated it as just another life event to be worked through, kind of like the tree that had fallen onto our house the year before. 'We'll get past this,' he would say. His gift of faith was amazing."

A Calling

Sitting in the Christmas Eve service that year (1999), a soloist sang "Immanuel," including the lyrics "If God is with us, who can be against us?" Mary was gripped by the deep meaning. "Love came down," she says. "I understood for the first time why Jesus came. He wanted to be in relationship with me. He came to restore what Satan had stolen in the Garden. It was a profound experience."

Something equally profound happened not long afterward when Mary—ever the activist—went to a Susan G. Komen "Race for the Cure." She remembers that "it was me and my bald head in the middle of 47,000 other people at the Southdale Mall, all wearing pink. Suddenly, in the midst of that event, I heard a voice deep in my spirit ... *I don't want you to race for them; I want you to PRAY for them.*

"Not that there was anything wrong with raising money for cancer research. But God was saying specifically to me that I should do something to merge the power of prayer with medical treatment. I had no idea how to do that. In fact, I had never prayed aloud in my life up to that point!"

She did nothing specifically about this calling for a while. But she did start reading her Bible with a ravenous thirst. She came to love 2 Corinthians 12:9—"He said to me, 'My grace is sufficient for you, for my power is made perfect in weakness.' Therefore I will boast all the more gladly about my weaknesses, so that Christ's power may rest on me" (NIV). She began letting that grace expand from herself to others, as she sat in the chemo-

> **"God was saying specifically that I should do something to merge the power of prayer with medical treatment. I had no idea how to do that."**

therapy chair for four hours at a time. She would look around the room and pray for her fellow sufferers.

At the Good Friday service that April, "my hair was starting to peek out a little bit, so that I looked like I'd had a crew cut. The actor who played Jesus that day began dragging a heavy cross down the center aisle. When he got to the front, and the sound of nails being pounded filled the sanctuary—I completely lost it. Jesus suffered that for me! I took a nail home from that service and taped it to my computer screen, so I'd never forget what he did for me. It's still there, in fact."

Pray for the Cure

Today, more than a decade later, Mary Nelson is vibrant and energetic; she even served a recent term as chair of Hosanna's executive body, our Vision Board. The members clearly recognize her as a leader. People especially know her as the founder of a monthly Monday night gathering in the prayer chapel called "Pray for the Cure." Here people with cancer come, often accompanied by family members and friends, to seek a shred of hope that maybe they'll have a future after all. Mary and her team of trained prayer ministers welcome them to the circle. Each person gets a brief chance to tell their latest medical status, challenges, and praise reports. But soon, Mary or another speaker moves into a teaching on the subject of healing. "We want to glorify God, not the enemy," she says. "I emphasize that it's more important to want Jesus than to want your healing. He heals us from the inside out."

Often a person who's now cancer-free gives their inspiring testimony. Then comes an extended time of individualized prayer. The format varies; some months the leaders use anointing oil, while other times they form prayer circles, and for still other nights there's what is called "soaking prayer," with soft lighting and soft music that sings the faith-filled words of Scripture. Each person receives the touch of one or more believers who call upon God for their restoration.

Widening Ripples

The word about Pray for the Cure has spread so widely now that cancer patients drive in from as far away as Wisconsin and Iowa for the meetings. Some obviously haven't been in church for years. Many have never had someone pray for them out loud. But the disease has thrown them into a place they never expected to be. They are now desperate. Attendance averages twenty to thirty, but has run as high as a hundred.

Jeremy and Lindsay Ginter showed up in the wake of their firstborn son, Evan, undergoing massive surgery for a PPB (pleuropulmonary blastoma)—an extremely rare but vicious lung tumor. He'd been a happy little baby for the first seven months of life, until at a Christmas gathering in 2008 his aunt said, "He seems to be breathing a little funny, don't you think?" The parents decided to have him checked by the pediatrician before heading out of town for the holiday with Lindsay's family in western North Dakota.

The pediatrician noticed that his chest seemed to pull up whenever he inhaled. So she decided to do an X-ray.

"When she put the film up on the light panel," Jeremy recalls, "there was this big black 'something' on his right lung. I thought, *Ahh, the machine goofed up.* The doctor said, 'Something's not right here at all. Let's do it again.'"

The second X-ray came out exactly the same.

Instantly the doctor sprang into high gear, giving the baby meds, applying an oxygen mask, and calling for an ambulance. Within the hour, the Ginters were at Children's Hospital, where specialists said the lung was being compromised by a large cyst. They thought it could be removed by surgery the day after Christmas without having to take the whole lung. Jeremy and Lindsay hugged each other and cried.

The three-hour surgery was successful, the lung reinflated, and little Evan came home on New Year's Eve. But then on January 12 came the pathology report: The "cyst" had actually been a PPB—something known only since the early 1980s, and present in fewer than 400 American children.

"What do we do now?!" the frightened parents asked each other. "Our baby has cancer!"

In addition to following medical advice, they began asking everyone they met to pray for their son. Jeremy had been raised Catholic and graduated from a Catholic university, "but I never really knew God and Jesus as a part of my life," he admits. "Lindsay had tried to get me to be more spiritual, and I'd put her off. But now ... I knew I needed to lean on God."

Searching online, they discovered Pray for the Cure. They showed up at the very next meeting. "We walked in a little cautiously," Lindsay says, "but we could quickly tell that everybody here was being very real, very honest about their battle. In going around the circle, it came our turn, and we tearfully told our story for the first time. People reached out to give us hugs."

The young couple was specifically prayed for that night—a new experience, but a welcome one. They came back the next month, and the next. "It made us stronger in our faith," Jeremy says. "I grew closer and closer to God, wanting to know more, reading more of the Bible. I found myself trying to convince my friends at work not to just spend their lives sitting back and 'hanging out,' but to take God seriously."

Lindsay adds: "In the early days after the diagnosis, I'd fallen into an attitude of 'Why us? We're not mean people. Why did this happen to our precious boy?' I have to say that Pray for the

Cure got me out of that. God did not choose us for this trial. This was not his plan by any means. He was instead the One who would step up to help us through it.

"The group helped me actually feel *blessed* that the cancer had been detected early, that surgery had been effective. Over time, we both came to know who it is that deserves gratitude. God had acted through medical expertise, and we will always thank him for that."

> **"A relationship with God should not just be driven by tragedy. We want to walk with him permanently."**

Evan has now been cancer-free for more than two years. The doctors keep doing PT scans, and apart from a few tiny spots that are staying unchanged, nothing else raises concerns. No further treatment has been prescribed. He's a normal, happy preschooler at this point. Jeremy and Lindsay, after genetic testing showed no risk, have become confident enough to have a second child.

"We keep praying over Evan as he sleeps in his crib," they say. "The prayer ministers at Pray for the Cure taught us that. And at one of the most recent meetings, they said to us, 'Okay, you guys, we're done praying over you two; you go and pray for some of the new people who are here tonight!' We'd never done that, and it was stretch for us to try. But we did.

"We've definitely changed. A relationship with God should not just be driven by tragedy. We want to walk with him permanently."

Into God's Hands

And so the healing power of God is multiplied from one person to the next. The kind of cancer patient who shows up at Pray for the Cure is often much older than little Evan Ginter—a man like, say, Bud Rother. This father of three and grandfather of three spent his whole working career in the electronics industry, working mainly on Defense Department contracts ... and just as the company offered him early retirement in January 2010, he started having physical problems. Was it just the stomach flu that was causing his dry heaves? No, a trip to the emergency room one Saturday revealed that his potassium level was off.

After admittance to a hospital, further tests showed low hemoglobin. And finally the culprit was identified: cancer in the bone marrow.

"They started chemo, which made me weak," he tells. "I was losing weight. I couldn't even go back to work to finish out my last few weeks before retirement. What was going to happen to me now?"

Bud had just begun to attend our church, participating in a class for new people called the Partnership Class. Now, he quickly got himself to the next Pray for the Cure. There he saw some men he knew from the Partnership Class. They gathered around to pray over him that night, spending several minutes interceding for God's help.

"Something completely changed right there," Bud says. "It was so uplifting. I went home and lay in bed that night, saying to the Lord, 'It's now in your hands. I can't do this by myself.'"

In the coming months, medical indicators showed definite improvement. His kidneys, which had initially been measured at only 5 percent efficiency, recovered enough for Bud to start stem cell replacement. His platelet count began to rise, and the hemoglobin held steady in an acceptable range. A few months later, the specialists released him back to the care of his regular physicians, writing a report that said, "Patient is in complete remission."

Says Bud: "The Lord has been overseeing this whole thing. That's why I keep going to Pray for the Cure. The prayers of so many people had a lot to do with my recovery. I tell people all the time: I don't think I'd have been healed without prayer. Being prayed over is just as important as going to the doctor."

Learning through Adversity

Mary Nelson smiles when she hears comments like this. They validate that the calling she received to *pray* for the cancer cure actually works. Other churches are now regularly asking her for guidance on how to set up a similar ministry in their settings, since cancer is so prominent these days. And she's glad to help (see www.maryjnelson.com).

In her book *Grace for Each Hour,* she writes, "It may seem odd to you, but I wouldn't trade my cancer experience for anything in the world. Why? Because there are certain things in this life that God can reveal to us only in the midst of adversity. There are hidden places deep in our souls He can reach only through our suffering. Here in the valley of weeping, in this secret place of refreshing springs where pools of blessing collect, we meet Almighty God face-to-face. What a privilege to stand in His courts!"[14]

Mary's comment is the echo of an ancient psalm. "A single day in your courts is better than a thousand anywhere else!"[15] The psalmist is saying (actually singing) that to be in God's presence and to experience his goodness is the *best.* One taste of that is better than a gourmet meal. One moment of that is better than a ten-day Caribbean cruise (and less fattening).

I think Mary spoke for a lot of us when she said, "God had my head, but he didn't have my heart." Faith is often seen as a belief system. If you believe this, that, and the other thing you can be on the team and sing in the choir. If you don't believe these things, you can't.

In other words, faith is a cognitive thing—something you think about and agree with, or not.

It all stays between your ears and has little to do with your heart and even less to do with experiencing him. Mary's cancer gave her a whole new understanding of faith. God's presence came upon her. That's what Immanuel means—"God with us."

If God is with us, for us, then nothing can defeat us. Not even cancer. It can get us down a little. It can make us bald. It can disrupt our lives. But it doesn't win. That's the promise that became real to Mary and the others when they experienced his presence.

Exactly how does that happen? Lots of ways, but there are two things I want you to see clearly in these stories.

"Alone" Doesn't Work

First, you have to let other people in. That's easy for me to write, but hard for me to do. I want to be responsible, solve problems, take charge, and *handle things myself.* I can still hear my dad saying those words over and over again. If there had been a Handle Things Yourself Club, he would have been president, and he would have passed out HTY buttons. I grew up wearing one and I thought that's the way it should be.

You know what the issue is? (I'm going to tell you, but only if you agree not to tell the members of my church. This is personal and I don't want them to know. Of course, if you tell them, I can handle it. Anyway ...) The issue is pride. I had to swallow mine to write that. Pride is an ugly wall we build around ourselves, and we don't like people trying to climb over the wall or even knocking on the little door in the wall. "Go away. I'm in here, but I can handle things myself."

Pride separates and isolates us from others. It keeps us away from one of God's primary healing ointments: people. In John Ortberg's book *God Is Closer than You Think,* he says people are God's main means of communication. God can send angels, put handwriting on a blank wall, whisper in a tiny voice, or speak through a donkey (you see that on TV once in a while), but more often than not he just likes to get through to us using family, friends, and, occasionally, a pastor or the guy waiting in line behind you. Amazing, really.

Cancer has a way of destroying that wall and letting others in. Not to trample around or feel sorry for us, but to serve, encourage, and love us. This brings a kind of healing that takes place right away, regardless of what the cancer is doing. I suppose pride is a type of cancer, but we know the cure for this one. Letting people in.

Pray vs. Say

The second think that is so obvious and critical in all these stories is prayer. I like Bud's quote, "Being prayed over is just as important as going to the doctor." Not more important, but just as important. What you want to do is get with people who pray prayers, not just say prayers. There's a difference.

At my first church I was the *associate pastor*. It's a title that means you've got your degree, but you don't really know anything. The title fit me perfectly. I was finally out of seminary (six years for me!—I wanted to get it right) and I was ready to preach sermons, baptize babies, and drink lots of coffee. These were three keys to effective ministry. And, if called upon, I could say a prayer.

In fact, we had a book of prayers, which we kept up at the front of the church. We'd read one of

I like Bud's quote, "Being prayed over is just as important as going to the doctor." Not more important, but just as important.

those prayers at the close of each service and then we'd put the date by it so we wouldn't pray it again too soon. We didn't want to bore God or let the people know that there were only thirty-two carefully prepared prayers to say. Occasionally I'd forget to bring the book out with me and, *holy Moses!* I'd have to pray a prayer. You know, like make it up, right on the spot. Two words describe those prayers: sweaty and short. God didn't seem to mind.

When I left that church to start Hosanna, I had to leave that prayer book behind. I had to learn how to pray prayers and not just say prayers. In Luke 11:1 one of the disciples asked Jesus to teach them. Not how to preach or how to raise money or how to keep it on the fairway. He said, "Lord, teach us to pray." He did. And he does.

Not long after we built our first Hosanna building I was told there was a couple who liked to come to our building on Sunday evening to pray. I didn't know them or invite them. They weren't even members of our church. But I wasn't going to track them down and say, "Hey, we don't do that around here." Soon six to eight others were joining in. Then a dozen. Then eighteen to twenty. Things were getting out of control.

Before I knew it, these "prayer people" were asking for a place to pray. A prayer chapel. We didn't have one, and I thought the idea would die quietly. One day our custodian came to me upset because all of his stuff had been put out in the hallway and there was a bunch of people in *his closet* praying up a storm. Our prayer ministry actually began in a janitor's closet that could hold about nine people, if they hadn't been on a Caribbean cruise (see previous paragraph).

Long story short, today at Hosanna we have about 220 partners who serve in our prayer ministry. They are divided into teams, and one team is on duty each time we worship. Before the service, they pray with the worship team and pastors. Then they go through the worship center

(2,500 seats) asking that the person who sits in each seat would receive a personal touch from God. They pray with people during the service in our Prayer Chapel and as worship is ending, they come down front to anoint and pray with those who come forward. On Wednesdays another team "covers" the building, when we have children and student ministries.

What Do You Expect?

Someone once told me that she thought Hosanna was an "expectant" church. What she meant was that when we pray, we expect things to happen. We do. And they do. We have healing stories and other miracles to celebrate almost every weekend. Migraines gone, pain diminished, anxiety relieved, marriages saved, fever broken, and tumors disappearing. Others experience oceanic peace or abiding hope or escalating joy.

So, you should go to God in prayer. That's what the Bible says: "Are any among you sick? They should call for the elders of the church and have them pray over them, anointing them with oil in the name of the Lord. And their prayer offered in faith will *heal the sick,* and the Lord will make them well. The earnest prayer of a righteous person has *great power* and *wonderful results*"[16]

In the first year of my ministry I went to see one of the saints in the hospital. Helen had suffered a heart attack and was recuperating slowly. I was nervous. What was I going to say to make her feel better? She was almost three times my age and had more spiritual maturity in her little finger than I had in my entire associate pastor body. So I fumbled around for words and shuffled my feet.

Finally, Helen said, "You're such a wonderful pastor. Thanks for coming to see me. I guess the Lord just wanted me to lie back and look up for a while."

For crying out loud. I was visiting her, and she was ministering to me, encouraging and thanking me. And then came that little pearl of wisdom, which I've not forgotten. From her hospital bed she was looking up to God. She wasn't angry or bitter or lonely. Her faith was at work and she was trusting God more than ever. "And we know that God causes everything to work together for the good of those who love God and are called according to his purpose for them."[17]

That verse doesn't say that God causes everything. Essentially it says that at all times, in all circumstances, God is at work—teaching, stretching, shaping, comforting, and healing those who love him. "Why me?" isn't the wrong question, but you might not get an answer to it for a while. It might be better to ask, "What are you trying to teach me, Lord? What do you want me to see? How can I trust you more?" These are questions he can answer in the moment, and the answers get woven into the fabric of healing.

I often say that the Lord does some of his best work when we are just outside of our comfort zone. I suspect the same is true when we are sick. When we look to him, he can turn dis-ease into a holy ease. And his comfort and compassion can become the foundation for a cure.

If you are in such a season, please let people in and ask them to pray for you. Those are the Lord's angels on assignment. They may bring presents (hopefully, dark chocolate), and you will experience his presence.

Enjoy both. Bless your heart.

9

TRAPPED

Certain topics are just, well, not meant for airing in "polite company"—which generally includes church. If your minister were to announce that next Sunday he'd be preaching on the subject of wife-beating, a lot of people would probably opt to spend the morning at Barnes & Noble instead.

But as a pastor, I can tell you that this issue is never far away. The ugly fact is that one out of every four women will suffer domestic violence sometime in her life. Each year an estimated 1.3 million American women get assaulted by an intimate partner.

It's a reality in my community, and yours. It's in our church. These women have come to my office, where in quiet tones they talk about the isolation and intimidation that haunt their daily existence. To speak up means risking even more abuse, they fear. But they desperately yearn for help in this dreadful area of their Monday-to-Saturday lives.

So I'm hoping this chapter might be a lifeline for some. While there is no humor here, there is hope. A number of women encouraged me to write on this topic. They have told me their stories.

They've been candid in terms of the harm they have experienced. And they have expressed the desire that in sharing their victory, their freedom, others might find a source of hope and a pathway out.

Unlike other chapters, there are no names here. Most women worry about their stories having ripple effects for children, extended family, friends, coworkers, and, yes, other church members. However, leaving the names out doesn't diminish what these women have lived through.

As I've listened, I've found many common threads to their stories, which are worth writing about. These are five of the major themes.

Craziness

For a woman living in an abusive relationship, there is nonstop turmoil. Her world seems to be upside down as she tries to navigate the treacherous waters of anger, tantrums, and intimidation. The abuser often has a Ph.D. in control and manipulation. He will do, say, or threaten whatever is necessary to maintain dominance in the relationship.

One woman told me her husband was always checking the odometer on her car to make certain she hadn't gone anywhere she wasn't "supposed to go." He would call her out of meetings to ask, yet again, when she would be coming home, and she could hear the kids crying in the background. Being out of the house was not an escape because the fear was so constant. What he would do while she was gone or when she returned was always on her mind and kept her walking on eggshells.

"The carpet had to be vacuumed a certain way, meals had to be served on time, and laundry needed to be folded and stacked." All of which she could do, but just when she would be putting forth every effort to appease him, he would change the rules or add some new demands. Weeks could go by with nothing being normal, no affirmation given, no tenderness offered.

For such women, all of this instability and anxiety starts to cause them to question their own sanity. "Most of the time I thought I was going crazy. Others seem to be getting by. Others are able to cope. Why can't I?" The craziness of her existence is no longer external, but starts to affect her mental and emotional health. Of course, he tells her she is crazy. And she slowly starts to believe it.

Isolation

People naturally question, "Why would any woman stay in this kind of hell? Why doesn't she stand up to him—or walk out?" Part of the answer is that the abuse has isolated her. She feels cut off from her own family, friends, neighbors, and most of the outside world. She might be functioning normally at work, at church, in the community, or as a mom, but boundaries have been so firmly established in her mind that she feels like she is living on an island.

Most communication has been cut off, curtailed, or controlled. He listens in on her phone calls and checks her messages. Her outings and activities have to be approved in advance. At family gatherings she is supposed to smile and be pleasant, acting as if all is well. In social settings he can be charming and funny, so no one has a clue as to his Jekyll-and-Hyde personality.

> **The ugly fact is that one out of every four women will suffer domestic violence sometime in her life.**

"I was amazed at who he would become when we were with other people," one woman told me. "He would tell great stories and make them laugh, often with his arm around me. I would laugh too, but inside I was aching and crying."

Another way he builds her isolation is by controlling the household finances. Often she is given only an allowance or kept on a very tight budget. She doesn't have her own money and is essentially dependent on him for all of her needs.

One of his most humiliating tactics is to tell her that she is fat or ugly or slow. There wouldn't be anybody to love her if he didn't. For one woman this humiliation began on the very first night of their honeymoon. The verbal and physical abuse became her reality for years to come. She had never felt so alone.

Feeling Overly Responsible

"If I love him enough and forgive him enough, he will change. I just have to try harder." Try harder.... Try harder.... Try harder.... An absolutely exhausting part of the relationship is the all-out effort the woman puts forth to be a better wife or girlfriend. She wants to please him and believes that there is a point, a level, a benchmark she needs to attain. When she does, he will be satisfied and the abuse will stop.

But there is no such point of breakthrough. Even if she thinks she sees it or knows it, he moves it ... and she, once again, falls just short of his satisfaction. She chases the proverbial carrot, but it remains just beyond her. His feelings of superiority and her feelings of responsibility fuel the violence.

Why does she want to please him? Why does she always feel responsible? *She loves him.* Most of us, when under any kind of attack, respond with either fight or flight. The outside hostility is met with our own hostility—certainly anger, sometimes violence. Or, we choose to remove ourselves from the threatening situation.

But not for the woman who *loves* her man. It's hard for most of us to understand how a woman can love a man who is abusing her. It changes all the dynamics. The Bible describes an unconditional love called, in Greek, *agape*. It is a choice and an act of the will. It doesn't come and go with changing feelings or circumstances. Often a woman in an abusive relationship has an amazing capacity to love. She has made a commitment to love for better or worse, and she wants to keep her word. So, she goes on loving him, feeling sorry for him, even while she hurts.

The Cycle

Another sound bite: "Sometimes when I was lying on the floor from getting slapped, he would suddenly blurt out, 'Will you forgive me? You know the Bible tell us we have to forgive, even seventy times seven. And if you don't, you're responsible to God.' So, in a quiet voice I would respond, 'Yes, I forgive you.'"

Abuse. Remorse. Apologies. Begging for forgiveness. Promises to never do it again. Forgiveness granted. Abuse.

This is the endless cycle in domestic violence. Often, just as the woman is coming to feel that she can't live like this one more day, he breaks down and starts to sob. Grief, regret, and remorse at what he has done seem to overwhelm him. He is ashamed, and out of that shame he asks for forgiveness. He almost demands it.

The begging is accompanied by sweeping promises to get help, be a better husband, and never do it again. Hope stirs once again within the woman. Maybe this is the answer to her prayers.

Maybe this is the turning point she has been waiting for. Maybe he really means it this time. Maybe.

But probably not. It's not that he doesn't mean it at some level. These feelings of shame or guilt aren't manufactured. It's as if a veil is briefly pulled back and he sees himself as the man he never wanted to become. The abuse he once experienced now defines him, and he is now the abuser. It shocks him, and so he promises to change.

The problem is that he is unable to break the cycle. He doesn't know how. He, too, is caught up in his own fears: fear of his past, fear of his insecurities. The abuser is often a perfectionist and can't face his own shortcomings and inabilities. This pattern is familiar to him. It probably has been for years, and so all the promises are soon broken. The cycle continues.

The Church

One woman told me this story: "A visiting minister came to our church, so I summoned the courage to ask for an appointment, seeking advice under the ruse of 'I work with women's ministry here. I'd just like your help on something. What do I tell women who are in a domestic abuse situation? How should I minister to them?'

"The minister replied, 'Well, I would suggest that you explain to them that marriage is a covenant. It's the same as a missionary being commissioned to go out to a foreign field. They do for God what they have pledged to do no matter what. Some of them actually die for their faith. It is the wife's responsibility to keep the covenant to love, respect, and honor the husband, even unto death.'"

The background of this situation was laid out as follows: "In our particular church culture nobody went to a therapist or psychiatrist for help. You just had to exercise more faith, pray more, and trust in God. I was told again and again that Jesus is our counselor."

I remember hearing one woman say, "I was allowed to read only Scripture passages my husband had approved and to hear only his interpretation of those verses. Sometimes he would awaken me in the middle of the night in a frenzy over the fact that I wasn't a submissive wife. I'd have to get down on my knees and repent that I wasn't good enough, didn't do enough, that I was just a horrible person. He would then go back to sleep, leaving me wide awake to stare at the ceiling wondering, 'Am I this bad, God? What more can I do?'

"Whenever there was a sermon at church on anger, I would cringe because I knew that as soon as we got home, he would say, 'You told him, didn't you?' He would feel convicted, and I would get beaten for the message, even though I had said not a word to the pastor."

Clearly, at times, the church has miserably failed women. The wrong message has been given about the meaning and dynamics of marriage. We have turned a blind eye to the scope of this issue while lifting up the marriage bond as the highest ideal. While I believe that marriage is for life, I also believe the Lord intended marriages to be a source of life, joy, intimacy, and trust.

When a marriage steals or diminishes or literally threatens life, there is no marriage. Vows have been broken, and intervention is necessary. The woman needs support, good counsel, and a plan. Her church should be a primary source of support, protection, and encouragement. She needs the assurance that the Lord can bring good out of her pain and brokenness.

Psalm for the Desolate

God has done just that for a number of these women. If you were to meet them now after reading their stories, you would find it hard to believe that they are the people in these stories. It seems like they should be broken, shy, wounded, fearful, and angry after that kind of abuse and trauma. Not so. Most of these women are bright, energetic, compassionate, and intelligent. One of my friends is at the top of her class in WOO – Winning Others Over. She really knows how to love people who are hurting.

These stories demonstrate the resilience of the human spirit and the healing power of God. "The darkness of those nineteen years was real, and most of the time I couldn't see the light. I couldn't imagine a way out of that living hell. I felt trapped. Then I read Psalm 55 and was astounded at how it described my situation. When it spoke of 'my enemy,' I personalized it to my situation":

> Listen to my prayer, O God.
>> Do not ignore my cry for help!
> Please listen and answer me,
>> for I am overwhelmed by my troubles.
> My (husband) shouts at me,
>> making loud and wicked threats.
> (He) brings trouble on me
>> and angrily hunts me down.
>
> My heart pounds in my chest.
>> The terror of death assaults me.
> Fear and trembling overwhelm me,
>> and I can't stop shaking.
> Oh, that I had wings like a dove;
>> then I would fly away and rest!
> I would fly far away—
>> to the quiet of the wilderness.
> How quickly I would escape—
>> far from this wild storm of hatred....
>
> It is not an enemy who taunts me-
>> I could bear that.
> It is not my foes who so arrogantly insult me-
>> I could have hidden from them.

Instead, it is you—my equal,
    my companion and close friend.
What good fellowship we once enjoyed
    as we walked together to the house of God.

Let death stalk my (husband);
    let the grave swallow (him) alive,
    for evil makes its home within (him).

But I will call on God,
    and the Lord will rescue me.
Morning, noon, and night
    I cry out in my distress,
    and the Lord hears my voice.
He ransoms me and keeps me safe
    from the battle waged against me,
    though many still oppose me...

As for my companion, he betrayed his friends;
    he broke his promises.
His words are as smooth as butter,
    but in his heart is war.
His words are as soothing as lotion,
    but underneath are daggers!

Give your burdens to the Lord,
    and he will take care of you.
    He will not permit the godly to slip and fall.

But you, O God, will send the wicked
    down to the pit of destruction.

Murderers and liars will die young,
    but I am trusting you to save me.[18]

My NLT Bible says the theme of this psalm is "expressing deep dismay over the treachery of a close friend. When friends hurt us, the burden is too difficult to carry alone." This is certainly true. But I have to think the deep dismay is multiplied times ten when the close friend is your spouse. It's one thing to have an external enemy, an adversary who wants to do us harm. But it's another thing entirely when the "enemy" is a spouse. The hurt is not only painful, but shocking and unwarranted.

In this connection, another Bible story comes to my mind. The book of Joshua tells about the nation of Israel entering the promised land and easily defeating the city of Jericho. Next was to be a little town called Ai. The spies who had gone ahead came back to tell Joshua that this would be an easy victory for the Israelites. Wrong. They were soundly beaten and "were paralyzed with fear at this turn of events, and their courage melted away."[19]

Well, Joshua cried out to God and suggested it might have been better if they had stayed back in Egypt rather than come out and get kicked around by the Amorites (a group of former ball players suspected of steroid use). The Lord told Joshua to knock it off and get his house in order. There was disorder and disobedience within the Israelite camp. In other words, the "enemy" causing all the problems was *in the camp.* A man named Achan had kept for himself some gold and silver that was supposed to be dedicated to the Lord. Bad news. He and his family were destroyed for their disobedience. The nation of Israel was once again free of fear and discouragement, and the conquest of the land continued.

Now I must tell you that I feel like I'm walking a tightrope right now. In this context, I don't want lots of spouses to read this and think "There's the answer. The person I'm married to is 'the enemy,' and I'm out of here." Not so fast. It takes two to make a good marriage, and it usually takes two to break a good marriage.

Nancy and I have gotten stuck a few times in our marriage. Stuck in unhealthy patterns of communication or noncommunication, or stuck in a time of misunderstanding and mistrust. This is when I would say "You're just like your mother," and her response would be "You're just like your father." She didn't see me as the enemy, but I wasn't at the top of her BFF list.

What do you do when your car gets stuck? You call a tow truck. When your marriage gets stuck—and most of them do—you call for help. Maybe it's a counselor, your pastor, your small group, or a wise friend. Swallow your pride and ask for good counsel.

Many years ago, Nancy and I saw a counselor, because I thought it would help her. After we talked quite a bit about my passive-aggressive tendencies, my perfectionism, and my controlling nature, she was doing much better. I have often thought we should go back for an annual check-up.

We have a powerful ministry at Hosanna called Rebuilders. It's designed to help couples who are stuck or whose marriages are broken down. We walk them through a step-by-step rebuilding process to recapture health, vitality, and trust in the relationship. The point is, many resources are available to those who are stuck and need help. Marriage was God's idea. He doesn't get us in only to watch us muddle

> *What do you do when your car gets stuck? You call a tow truck. When your marriage gets stuck— and most of them do—you call for help.*

through. So pray, plan, open up, seek, ask, and receive.

Back to the tightrope analogy. I don't want to be the cause of more broken marriages ... "This guy wrote a book and he said you were the enemy. So long." On the other hand, I'm hoping that a number of women who read this chapter might see themselves and might also begin to see a light at the end of a long, dark tunnel.

So now I want to write directly to you who are in an abusive relationship. "The enemy" is in your camp. He's in the bed with you. Yes, he's your partner, but he has stolen from you. Health, security, confidence, freedom, and joy are gone, or fleeting at best. The cause of your misery is not the circumstances in which you find yourself. The cause is the relationship in which you are trapped.

You are not going crazy. Yes, there seems to be no way out—usually due to the presence of children and/or the lack of finances. You feel tremendous responsibility for the children as well as almost total dependence on him for support. These circumstances seem to be the bars on your jail cell.

Still, you can express your feelings as the psalmist did:

"Pull me from the trap my enemies set for me, for I find protection in you alone."[20]

"Although I did them no wrong, they laid a trap for me. Although I did them no wrong, they dug a pit for me."[21]

"My enemies have set a trap for me. I am weary from distress."[22]

Even King David, a mighty warrior and a man after God's own heart, felt the despair, loneliness, and exhaustion of dealing with those who sought to do him harm.

Perhaps others have tried to be helpful by offering explanations for your husband's behavior. They've said it has to do with his history ... there was abuse in his family ... his dad drank a lot ... his mother was involved with other men. Or there is a diagnosable mental issue ... he's bipolar, but he does pretty well when he stays on his meds. Or it's psychological ... he has passive-aggressive tendencies exacerbated by his obsessive compulsive disorder.

Well, while some or all of that may be true, explanations can never serve as excuses. There is no excusing abusive behavior. Just because it can be understood does not mean it should then be tolerated. Although you may not feel like it much of the time, you are the healthier one and you will need to break the cycle.

Three Truths

Let me make three assertions that I believe with all my heart:

1. *You have done nothing to deserve this.* Of course, he says you have, and he points out all of your faults and shortcomings. Granted, none of us is perfect—but his anger and abuse are never justified by your humanity. Every one of us needs a nurturing community, not endless correction.

177

2. *You are not his property.* You are his *wife,* which is a description of the relationship, not a claim of *possession.* When God created Eve he said she would be Adam's *helper.* Every other time that the same Hebrew word is used in the Old Testament, it refers to God. In other words, Eve was to help Adam just as God would. Help him what? Build a relationship with communication, compassion, intimacy, and joy. She was not his possession. She was his partner.

3. *You are worthy of being loved.* Love is an act of the will; it is a choice we make. It is often accompanied by feelings of affection or romance, but not always. How else could Jesus tell us to love our enemies?[23] The love you have for your husband speaks to the beauty and tenderness of your heart. But *you also deserve and are worthy of just such a love.* The Scripture says so clearly: "And you husbands must love your wives and *never treat them harshly."*[24]

My desire for you is healing and then hope. The physical and emotional injuries that you have experienced are just as traumatic and serious as those experienced in a bad car accident. You are not surprised when an ambulance leaves the scene of an accident and rushes a patient to the emergency room. Similarly, there are those who would come to your rescue and assist you so that the healing might begin.

The First Step Is to Ask

But they can't step in, won't step in, until you ask for help. I know it seems risky, but it's the first step in breaking the cycle. Is there a family member, a dear friend, a pastor, a doctor, or a women's shelter? These people and resources will provide you with security, healing, good counsel, and a plan.

Most often, the only way of getting out is to let someone in. Let their strength and compassion be yours in the early going.

Soon you will again feel hopeful. No one lives well or long without hope. When I talk about "getting out," I'm talking about getting out of the abuse, not necessarily getting out of the marriage. Any marriage can be restored if both people want it to happen. You don't have to abandon him, but you are declaring that you will not go on in the old relationship. Even as you seek health and wholeness, he needs to do the same.

If he chooses not to, there is no marriage to be saved. Marriages are based on the promises (vows) made by a man and a woman. A relationship can be restored and even made stronger when both people renew and keep those promises. But no relationship can be built on broken promises and shattered trust.

There is a lasting hope that comes from the Lord:

"Those who live in the shelter of the Most High
will find rest in the shadow of the Almighty.
This I declare of the Lord:
He alone is my refuge, my place of safety;
he is my God, and I am trusting him."[25]

The women I have quoted in this chapter have moved from tragedy to triumph. Once trapped in the pit of abuse, they have been set free. Healing and hope have come their way.

This is what the Lord has in mind for you. Just as there is joy in his house on Sunday, he wants joy in your house, in your heart, on Monday and all the days of your life.

10

A NEW SEASON

When I tell people I've lived in Minnesota all of my life they usually pat me on the shoulder and say, "That's okay." It's like I could have gone to the Caribbean, but I chose a Caribou coffee instead. Or, instead of riding the trains all over Europe with Nancy, I took the LRT downtown with Ralph to watch the Twins get hammered by the White Sox. Again. The pat on the back and sad look somehow convey that I have blown it by living here. Who in their right mind would choose that?

I don't think anyone outside of Minnesota is going to read this book, so we can talk openly among ourselves. (If you are a resident of another state, please skip down to paragraph #9.)

The Real Reason

We know why we live here. Is it the politics? We did elect Jesse Ventura as our governor (I didn't dream that, did I?). Two different Minnesotans initially threw their hat into the ring for U.S. President in 2011.

Or is it our education system? All of our children are adorable and bright. They speak at least two languages, English and Fargoese, and every one of them can play some instrument in the marching band.

Or is it our 10,000-plus lakes—each one full of fantastic walleyes and friendly game wardens? Every Minnesotan owns a boat or has a brother-in-law who does.

Or is it our professional sports teams? See paragraph #1.

We know why we really live here. It's the *changing seasons.* Outsiders think we have only winter and one other season in which we get ready for winter. Fine, let 'em think that. We know we have four distinct, beautiful seasons, and this proves we are God's favorites. "As long as the earth remains, there will be springtime and harvest, cold and heat, winter and summer, day and night."[26] There is a rhythm and variety in God's creation, and you see it best in Minnesota. You'll never confuse Duluth with Phoenix.

There's nothing like the sun glistening on the sky blue waters of one of our lakes. My mother used to say it looks like a million diamonds (which you wouldn't say to "other people" because you wouldn't want them to think you were rich or hoity-toity). Then comes the panorama of the fall colors. We take car trips up to the North Shore just to see the colors at their peak. How about a gentle snowfall on Christmas Eve? I've seen Christmas lights on palm trees, and that's just plain wrong. Then comes the sighting of your first robin in the spring, and you know it's time to sharpen the lawn mower blade. Four seasons, just like God intended. Perfect.

Bucking the Routine

Now, allow me to welcome back our readers from California (I have five friends out there plus my brother and sister-in-law). We are talking about the seasons of life (which is a funny thing to say because nobody's talking—I'm writing and you're reading). Everybody knows we all go through seasons or stages in life. Something like this:

- Diapers
- Pre-school
- Real school
- College and partying
- Move back in with your parents
- WORK!
- Lose weight or have prostate surgery
- Write a book
- Die

Some people write the book before they have the surgery, which is what I've chosen to do, but this is pretty much how it goes. So what's the problem?

There are several problems with this scenario. For lots of people it's not a wonderful rhythm for life, but rather a rigid routine. Dullsville. They want to bungee-jump or hang-glide, or the wildest ones want to live in Manhattan. They don't want life to be predictable.

Other people realize this is how it's supposed to be, but they are actually stuck in one of these seasons. They just don't believe their parents would actually evict them.

Here's why I don't like this scenario, even though I wrote it. The word *new* can be found over 300 times in the Bible. It's even got a *New* Testament. You can hardly go two pages without reading about a new song, a new generation, new strength, or new wine. New life is available to each one of us, and eventually we each get a new body! That's fine by me. I'm getting one without any weird age spots or bald spots. The very last time the word is seen in the Bible is when Jesus says, "Look, I am making all things new!"[27]

> **Do you get the idea that God isn't into routines or reruns? I'll bet he's never watched a movie more than once.**

Do you get the idea that God isn't into routines or reruns? I'll bet he's never watched a movie more than once, except for *The Hunt for Red October,* which is every-body's favorite. If that's his nature and we belong to him, doesn't it follow that he probably wants to do new things in our lives? Things that stretch us, grow us, teach us, test us, and change us. In fact, it seems like that would be the norm, rather than some boilerplate routine. We should be on the lookout for new opportunities and the next adventure. It probably won't be skydiving, although I highly recommend that. It almost certainly will be something that brings the best out of me, blesses others, and makes God smile.

Branching Out

That's certainly what happened to my friend Bob Swan and the Joy in his life. This couple was on a good glide path: accomplished, fruitful, productive, well-respected, and content. Add to this beautiful children with straight white teeth about to enter their reproductive years, lots of friends, nice house, and they belonged to a fantastic church. Everything was in order ... until God opened up a new door, which led to a new season.

As KLM Royal Dutch Airlines continued ramping up its alliance with Northwest Airlines in 1998, thousands of jobs got consolidated—including Bob's. He had served KLM for 27 years, starting in his native Ontario, then moving on to Atlanta, New York, Houston and finally Minneapolis, where he was general manager of the Central Region. Now, at age 52, he'd need to look for something else.

"Joy and I weren't particularly upset," he says with his warm smile, "even though our girls were just getting to the wedding stage of life, and it was an expensive time for us. But I knew the travel industry pretty well. It wasn't long before I went back to work for a wholesaler named Borton Overseas. We put together international packages—air, ground transportation, lodging, daytime excursions—that local travel agents would market to honeymooners and other well-heeled vacationers. Corporations would use our services, too, to reward their high achievers."

One of the exotic destinations, of course, was Africa, with its fascinating safaris. Bob made his first scouting trip in 2000. He was scheduled to go again in the fall of 2001, and this time Joy went along as well. "We were the advance team for a group of automotive salespeople who had won some contest," Bob explains. "We would escort them to see the wild game of South Africa and Botswana, winding up at Victoria Falls on the Zambia-Zimbabwe border," the largest single sheet of falling water in the world.

But the tourists—scheduled to fly from the U.S. on September 16—obviously never got off the ground, due to the tragedy of 9/11. Bob and Joy, already in place, were left to explore the sights for themselves. "We began to see the real Africa for the first time," Bob recalls. "I stood watching laborers hauling bricks in rickety wheelbarrows all day to earn maybe 50 cents, and I couldn't quite take it. We watched children in ragged clothes pawing through garbage piles for food. Our hearts began to be broken."

Joy had always been a lover of children, "whether my own three girls, my son, or others. For a while, I had done courier work, bringing Korean babies across the ocean to be adopted in the U.S. So for me, the African scene was more of the same thing I'd always cared about."

Attitude Shift

But her husband was undergoing a major attitude shift. "In the travel business, you're always playing the angles to get a perk," he admits. "You know how the systems work, you're friends with certain people, and you're always focusing on 'How can I get an upgrade?' You never want to settle for coach class; you never want to have to pay normal rate for a hotel room. On the long flight down to Cape Town, in fact, I'd managed to get first-class seating for Joy and me. It was very comfortable, of course.

"And now I was standing here seeing people who could never hope to get *any* seat on *any* airplane in their whole lives. They'd be lucky to come up with bus fare instead of having to walk. A whole different sensitivity was gradually burrowing into me. God was gradually turning up the rheostat of passion in my heart."

Back home in Minneapolis that winter, Bob enrolled in a two-year leadership training program at our church called "The Potter's Wheel." It explores how God might wish to reshape your life and talents for the purposes of his kingdom. One of Bob's course requirements was to get out of the classroom and go research, conceptualize, and design an actual mission program of some kind. It includes setting a strategy and showing how you're going to measure results.

Bob Swan decided to focus on East Africa. "The day after Christmas 2003, I hopped on a plane (yes, I got into business class!) and flew all night to Amsterdam, then all day until landing around 10 p.m. at Kilimanjaro International Airport in northeast Tanzania. I didn't have any pre-arranged schedule; I was simply going to explore, with the help of a driver from a safari company I knew.

"I stepped out into the dark African night—almost no lighting in the parking area—and wondered for a moment what I'd gotten myself into. But the driver stepped out from the shadows holding a little sign with my name on it. Whew! He took me an hour up the road to downtown Arusha, where I went to bed in a small cabin inside a walled compound ... listening to a group of Masai tribal teenage boys whooping it up, trying to amp up their courage for the next morning's circumcision ceremony. In the trees, birds kept making noise as well. And then around 5 a.m., the nearby mosque's loudspeakers began blaring the Muslim call to prayer. This was definitely not the Sheraton campus!"

For the next set of days, Bob and his driver began exploring the countryside, looking for needs that a Hosanna work team might fill. Eventually he found a roadside clinic building twelve kilometers out of town that the government had never gotten around to finishing. As a result, villagers continued to suffer, women went on delivering their babies at home with little assistance, and children kept dying of common conditions (diarrhea, for example) that were easily preventable. This would make a good project.

Bob came home, wrote up his strategic plan, recruited eleven people, and left for Africa three months later. Handling the trip logistics—reservations, passports, visas, security arrangements, etc.—was, of course, right up his alley. The group spent ten days getting the clinic in shape—and along the way, attended a town church on Sunday.

Before they knew it, a delegation from the church came out to the work site and invited them to a special lunch. More than just sandwiches and drinks, the lunch turned out to be a full spread at another church nearby that was little more than sticks with mud (or dung) plaster. The rural pastor was a precious soul, and when the workers asked him about the half-finished edifice they saw next door, he answered sadly, "That was going to be our real sanctuary. But then the drought came, and we never gathered enough money to keep building." Instantly, Bob and his group knew what their second project should be.

189

Our "Bwana"

Since that launch in March 2004, Bob has been back to Africa at least sixteen times, often leading some of the 350 to 400 of our people in mission endeavor. Joy has been at his side many of the trips as well. He is now our volunteer director for African ministry, so much that we teasingly call him *"Bwana"* (Swahili for "master" or "boss").

His understandings of God's purposes for this part of the world have deepened over time. "We felt God was saying to us, 'If these countries are ever going to move forward, you have to reach the children while they are young, so they can grow up to be strong leaders, untainted by despair or corruption.' So our focus has become a three-legged stool:

1. Look after their *hearts* (by building churches, Sunday schools, providing curriculum, etc.)
2. Look after their *bodies* (by developing medical services, clinics, bringing supplies, etc.)
3. Look after their *heads* (by building schools, houses for teachers, etc.)"

Joy adds, "We began to feel that we should return multiple times to the same places, so they would know we hadn't forgotten about them. Some Africans told us, 'Nobody seems to come back. They may send some money from time to time, but they're not really engaged with us.' We came to believe that return contact was vital to deepening relationships. That's why we've kept going back to northeast Tanzania."

Bob continues: "This is a twenty-year investment, to take little five-year-olds and produce leaders out of them. You can't just squirt some money at the situation and run off.

"But when you look into these children's eyes, you can see the intelligence. They are so full of life. They're so hopeful. There's a flame you want to fan."

It was a full three years before the Swans, on one of their trips, ventured to explore a second area for ministry: neighboring Malawi. This small country to the south was a tougher challenge in some ways, because so many adults seemed to be missing due to AIDS, or malaria. They found tons of children and teenagers, and lots of overburdened grandparents—but a demographic hole in the middle.

"We were staying at a nice camp in a national park (I'd gotten it free!)," Bob remembers, "when they took us across a river full of alligators to see a 'school.' It was little more than a thatched roof held up by poles. Right away, I just sensed inside that God wanted us to strengthen that school.

"The further we walked down that dirt road, the more kids began to clamor around us. We felt such a connection with them. Then, off the road and back in the tall grass, I spotted an empty building. What was this? It turned out to be another medical clinic, with four staff houses around it—all standing empty! The facility had been built four years previous, but for some political reason it was now abandoned.

"We came back to Hosanna talking about it and saying, 'We've *got* to get this clinic up and running.' The church caught the vision. So did some outside donors, from as far away as Cleveland. Today it's serving the people of that area, and so is the nearby school. There's a young Presbyterian pastor there who is leading the overall ministry for the glory of God."

I could go on and on, telling about the Swans' efforts in leading forgiveness-and-reconciliation meetings among African groups long estranged from one another. Here in the Twin Cities, some Ethiopian refugees heard them speak and were so moved that they said, "You *have* to go teach this material to our people back in Ethiopia. They need this so badly." That has come to pass, with remarkable healing as a result. Audiences in Burundi and Uganda have been impacted as well.

Full Speed Ahead

Bob and Joy, now soaring through their sixties, show no signs of slowing down, or of settling for a typical American retirement. "This era has opened our eyes to see that life is about a whole lot more than just us," says Bob. "Whatever we have in terms of skills or contacts or funds, Jesus wants us to be his servants, to walk around looking for people to bless. In fact, he empowers Christians to do that. And we will always be thankful for other leaders, such as Jan and Terry Lyman, for helping lead the way in Africa.

"My favorite Scripture is John 14:12, where Jesus said, 'Very truly I tell you, whoever believes in me will do the works I have been doing, and they will do even greater things than these, because I am going to the Father.' He wasn't exaggerating; it's true! We feel privileged to have the freedom to

> *"Whatever we have in terms of skills or contacts or funds, Jesus wants us to be his servants, to walk around looking for people to bless."*

do what God has laid on our hearts to do, within a frame-work of accountability. This is the best life we can imagine."

I love it when words spoken by Jesus become a photo caption or an article headline. If you saw a picture of Bob and Joy or read a story about them, somewhere you could well see the words "Even Greater Things." It's hard for many people to imagine that Jesus really meant what he said. How can we do even greater things than he did? He was Jesus, the Son of God. Yes he was, so he probably knew what he was talking about. Plus, the one who wants to work in and through us is the Holy Spirit—the same person and the same power that raised Jesus from the dead. Seriously.

You've heard the story about the little boy trying to lift a heavy object, and he couldn't do it. His dad wanted to teach him something important, so he told his son, "Use all of your strength." The boy assured his dad that he was. "Use all of the strength you have," the dad said again. The boy was exasperated and not too happy with the repeated advice. "I am, Dad!" he insisted. Then came the important lesson: "No, Son, you're not using all the strength you have until you ask me to help. My strength is available to you anytime you want it." The heavy box was then moved easily and the lesson was learned.

Bob and Joy were tuned into the presence and power of the Holy Spirit before Africa. They were wonderful people of faith, servant leaders at Hosanna. But something happened when Bob had to get out of the Potter's Wheel classroom. He brought this to the Lord in prayer, and I suspect the Lord smiled because he can always do great things through an open heart and available hands.

He used the Swans' good marriage, their international travel expertise, their faith, their love of children, and their sense of adventure. He took all of that and then applied divine math. With God it's always multiplication, not just simple addition. In other words, you give God 3 and 3 and he's not going to come out with 6, like we would. He comes out with at least 9 ... and sometimes it's 27, because he is a triune God and so he enters his own 3 into the equation. It's the new math for a new season.

You might think I'm making this up, but how else do you feed 5,000 hungry people with two fish and five little loaves of bread? We would have come up with four fish fillet sandwiches and some breadsticks. The Lord satisfied the whole crowd and had leftovers for the in-laws. Multiplication.

Faith for Heavy Lifting

Did you also notice that the Swans had to flex that faith muscle? First Bob, then Joy. The muscle wasn't flabby for either one of them, but it wasn't fully developed. It never is for any of us. When they set out to do some heavy lifting, the Father added his strength, and big dreams became a reality. A mission became a movement. The faith muscle grew in a lot of people.

I think this is a good lesson for all of us. I know that my faith muscle becomes flabby when I'm simply doing what is familiar and comfortable. Faith then becomes a little like insurance—I'm glad I have it, but I hope I don't need it.

However, when I'm willing to try something outside my comfort zone or beyond my natural abilities, faith moves from being insurance to being assurance. I'm trusting the assurance that the Lord has given to me. King David spoke the words of assurance when he said to his son, "Be strong and courageous, and do the work. Don't be afraid or discouraged by the size of the task, for the Lord God, my God, is with you. He will not fail you or forsake you."[28]

That's more than just a nice Bible verse. When we are willing to risk something for God, it can transform from being a Sunday thought to a Monday reality. That doesn't mean we are headed to Africa—which is the proverbial fear: "If I let God have his way with me, he'll send me to East Podunk to be a missionary." Probably not (but did you know that the East Podunkers know more about community and hospitality than you do?). The point is not Africa or even south Minneapolis. The point is trusting God enough to adopt a mission mindset and seeing all of life as a faith adventure.

> *You don't want your memories to exceed your dreams; that's when you get old and should start shopping for a walker.*

At Hosanna we often send worshipers off with this thought: "You are going on a great mission trip this week. It could be in your neigh-borhood, your classroom, the cubicle next to you at work, or the local hardware store. Look for and listen for God. There will be any number of divine opportun-ities to serve, help, en-courage, rescue, or listen to others." The whole congregation should be a mission team *every week,* and our collective faith muscle should make Arnold Schwarzenegger look like Mr. Whipple (please don't squeeze the Charmin).

You may be feeling like you have missed out on things, or you've failed to take a chance, or your life is just plain ordinary, or it's simply too late. Here's my pastoral word for you: *Baloney.* That's why I like the Swans' story so much. Their lives weren't dull—but God was ready to do a new thing with them and usher them into a whole new season. That's what he has in mind for every one of us right now.

A Word for Baby Boomers

You know that wimpy saying "Be patient with me—the Lord isn't finished with me yet." It sounds like an excuse for mediocrity or a procrastinator's T-shirt. I think we should be saying, *"Watch Out— the Lord Has More in Store for Me."* You don't want your memories to exceed your dreams; that's when you get old and should start shopping for a walker. I always feel that with God, *the best is yet to come.* That which we have seen and experienced is just a foretaste of even greater things ahead.

You haven't missed out, and it's not too late. I want to direct this comment especially to Baby Boomers. I am one, and I want to include just a few thoughts here because they don't fit in the chapter on sex. There are 76 million of us. Because of our sheer numbers we have redefined music, youth, rights, clothing, travel, medicine, and now aging. We are the wealthiest and best-educated generation of Americans ever. We can also be kind of whiny.

When commentators talk about the graying of America, they are talking about us. Most of the time it sounds like we are going to become a real load for this nation. And we will, with our needs (demands) for Medicare, Social Security, assisted living, and end-of-life care, even as we live longer than any previous generation. The government has made promises it can't keep.

Are you still reading this, or are you sending me an ugly e-mail? I want to remain pastoral and not become political. I'm simply saying that we have been leaders in so many ways, and now is the time for the best kind of leadership. Let that come from us Boomers. We can live by fear or by faith, and there is a lot of fear in our country right now.

To my fellow Boomers I say: The circum-stances are very challenging, even frightening, just now. That's true economically, politically, socially, and globally. If we focus only on our retirement years, our needs and demands, wondering if there's enough *for us,* we'll live in fear and we won't finish well.

However, if we believe the best is yet to come … if we see retirement not as the last season but the new season … we can still accomplish greater, lasting things. It will require boldness, faith, sacrifice, and trust. But the results will be blessings of biblical proportions. The opportunity is ours and the time is now. Again, it's not too late.

There's a lot of evidence that people don't do their best work until they're 80:

- Moses was 80 and Aaron was 83 when they first got in Pharaoh's face. And, BTW, "Moses was 120 when he died, yet his eyesight was clear, and he was as strong as ever."[29] He could still trim his own nose hair and then lift a block of salt up into the water softener (a couple of my own measures for good health).
- Daniel was 80 when they threw him into the lions' den.
- Ben Franklin was 81 when he helped draft the Constitution, and he was probably still flying kites.
- Justice Oliver Wendell Holmes, Jr., was in his 80s when he wrote some of his classic legal opinions, and he served into his 90s. He wasn't sitting on the bench, he was serving on the bench.

The author of Psalm 92 got it right:

It is good to give thanks to the Lord....
It is good to proclaim your unfailing love
in the morning,
your faithfulness in the evening....
You thrill me, Lord, with all you have done

199

for me!...
You have me as strong as a wild bull.
How refreshed I am by your power!...
The godly will flourish like palm trees...
Even in old age they will still produce fruit;
they will remain vital and green.[30]

That's what I'm talking about. God has new things in store for you and me, and the best is yet to come. So I'm going to finish this book even though I'm 441 in dog years, and then I'm going to buy a Harley. Don't tell Nancy.

11

SOMEONE'S DAUGHTER

I remember the first time I saw a *Playboy* magazine. I suppose I was nine or ten at the time, and my dad had come home for lunch. He owned a painting/contracting business and thus had a flexible schedule. At that particular moment he was maybe on the phone or talking to a neighbor, but he wasn't around—and there was this magazine lying on our kitchen counter. I didn't know what it was.

A page was folded back, so I opened it up to see what was marked. I quickly recognized one of the ads from something I'd seen during a trip to visit relatives in Florida. We had gone to the beach, and on that day there were cameras and lights set up for some kind of photo shoot. A man was sitting in a comfortable chair, and two women were serving him some kind of drink.

Why did it take two women to serve one guy a drink? My logical mind was clicking. And why were they dressed in costumes and he wasn't? Rabbit ears, cotton tails, and high-heeled shoes— on the beach! A nice little crowd of beachgoers seemed pretty interested in watching. I didn't get it at all; I was ready to swim.

Now in my kitchen, that was the picture I recognized in the *Playboy* ad. No wonder the magazine was in our house. I flipped through to see if I recognized any other pictures ... holy cow! I couldn't believe what I was looking at, and I don't know if my heart or my mind raced faster. About 150 beats per minute and at least that many thoughts. Thoughts like *Wow ... I'd better tell my dad.... I hope my dad doesn't come in right now.... Who else knows about this?... Who are these women?... Why would they do this?... Why are my palms sweaty?*

But the overriding thought or feeling was *I'm going to get caught.* Of course, you never worry about "getting caught" unless you are doing something wrong. So, right away I knew there was something wrong about this. I shouldn't be doing this. When I heard my dad coming, the magazine went back on the counter. I never saw it or any one like it in the house again.

But I obviously haven't forgotten that experience.

Intimacy or Idiocy

In the Creation story God paused at the end of each day to admire his own work. Without exception he liked what he saw, and he said so. "This is good."[31] That changed, however, when he saw Adam by himself—even though Adam had the whole world to enjoy. He could go horseback riding, walk on the beach, grill man food, and watch all the football he wanted. And he didn't have to give a thought as to what outfit he was wearing. Still, God said, "This is not good."[32] He knew just what Adam needed, and it wasn't another cordless drill.

While Adam was sleeping (God knew his nap schedule), God created Eve. Now imagine Adam waking up and seeing Eve for the first time. She wasn't a centerfold, but the dress code was the same. He blurted out, "At last! She is part of my own flesh and bone! She will be called 'woman,' because she was taken out of a man."[33] Essentially he shouted, *"Now that's what I'm talkin' about! Can I have this dance?"* He liked what he saw.

And ever since then, men have had choices: intimacy or idiocy, pleasure or power, honoring or abusing, admiration or addiction. When we teach the kids at Hosanna about sex-ual desire, we liken it to fire. Sexual desire is one of God's most amazing gifts to each of us. But, like any passion or desire, it needs some boun-daries.

> *You never worry about "getting caught" unless you are doing something wrong.*

Fire in a fireplace gives warmth, beauty, and enjoyment. Fire unguarded or unbounded can burn down the whole house.

This is a chapter about pornography—an issue for both men and women. I will write from a

203

male perspective, but all that I write is true for women as well.

I could tell countless stories about unbridled sexual desire destroying relationships, health, careers, and self-esteem. The house burned to the ground, and the loss was total. I'm not just talking about perverts or drug addicts. Over the years I have dealt with this danger with many church members, with our leaders, even with our staff. My opinion is that it is escalating in its reach and destructive power.

Pick any two men you happen to know; statistics say one of them has looked at pornography in the last thirty days. A certain pastor thought that couldn't possibly be true in his church. It wasn't—the percentage was closer to 60 percent. "Sexual addiction" is a term that has only been used in the last twenty-five years, but it is accurate, because the evil and the outcomes are the same as any other addiction. Books are now being written on causes, costs, and cures.

I'm grateful that a handful of men agreed to speak to me directly. I'll tell one of their stories and weave in thoughts or insights from some of the others.

Lessons Delayed

Growing up in a small town an hour and a half south of here, Mark[†] learned some good lessons. He learned to work hard and not be lazy; after all, his dad had earned his way up to superintendent of a manufacturing plant. Mark also learned to keep track of your hat and gloves through the long winter so you don't get frostbite ... to sit still and behave in church on Sunday morning ... to defend yourself in a house with three older brothers.

Unfortunately a couple of other lessons got skipped along the way. One was the power and hazard of alcohol. The other was to respect and value females. "My mom—the only woman in a house full of guys—was very much controlled by my dad," Mark remembers. "She couldn't do much of anything or go anywhere without his permission. One time when he did let her go out of town for some event with the church women's group ... he openly took us boys along with him to go visit his mistress! He told us not to tell our mother."

Today, at age forty-four, Mark has learned both those lessons. And in both cases, God used a certain kind of instructor to drive them home—a cop.

Drinking started when Mark was in eighth grade. By college, there was little restraint at the

---

[†] See explanatory note on page 4.

bar. After two years, his studies weren't really going that well, so he decided to head for the Air Force instead, where he became a security specialist. "I really liked the military—enough to want to make a career of this," he says. "I felt proud of myself. In fact, my dad shocked me one day by saying he was proud of me, too. I'd never heard that."

After postings in Texas and New Jersey, he got the chance to go to Germany. Mark was excited about this adventure—and all the more when he landed to find out that the special at Burger King was comprised of a Whopper, fries, and a beer. Sweet! He had never imagined such a convenient arrangement.

He also soon discovered the brothel down the road. Prostitution was entirely legal in Germany. "I thought I'd landed in heaven," he says today with chagrin. "My idea of love was so distorted. I thought *love* was just another word for sex. Here in this setting, I didn't need to build any kind of a relationship with a woman. I could just 'keep it simple.'"

Dumped

Things weren't so simple, however, when it came to the Air Force's rule on alcohol-related incidents: Three strikes within a year's time, and you're out. Mark managed to use up his quota within six months. He was discharged and shipped back to the States.

"I was very hurt by this," he says. "The world was suddenly falling down around my shoulders. What would I do next? When I called home to tell what had happened, my dad roared, 'I'm so embarrassed by you! I don't care if I ever see you again. Don't bother coming here—that's for sure!'"

So he stayed with a brother for a while, until he got a job in St. Cloud, Minnesota, working for a construction company. His drinking accelerated, up to four nights a week. "And once I started with one drink, there was no backing off," he says. "I felt sorry for myself. The 'liquid courage' gave me confidence, I thought."

While in nearby Sartell for a softball tournament, he met his future wife in a bar. Neither one of them was entirely sober at the moment. After two years of partying together, they got married in 1992. She had issues of her own, and "I didn't know how to help her or respect her. She wanted to go to church, though, so I tagged along a few times. I didn't get anything out of it, though."

Then came Memorial Day weekend 1995. The young couple spent the day drinking at a relative's backyard party, then headed to a bar in the evening. "Some stranger was talking to my wife, and I took offense," Mark admits. "I caused a scene, started a fight—and in order to get at the guy, I grabbed my wife by the throat and pushed her out of the way. Soon the police were called, and I was in handcuffs for 'domestic assault.' I landed in jail that night, totally humbled."

Sitting in his cell with nothing to do but think, Mark reviewed his life so far. His major problems had stemmed from alcohol, hadn't they? He made a bold decision that day: No more drinking, period. The courts eventually had him go to anger management class as well as Alcoholic Anonymous. Now eighteen years later, he can say he has kept his pledge. "By the grace of God I haven't had a drink since."

A Void to Fill

Things at home improved for a while, to the point that a little boy, Owen, was born in 1998. But tensions resumed, and the couple experienced more arguments than joy as time went on.

"One night in 2001, I came home from work—and the house was empty. I had no idea where they had gone. The next day, however, she called and said she would let me have Owen half of the time."

A divorce was finalized the next year. Mark stuck to his pledge not to drink. But he yearned for an intimate touch, and eventually he started using dial-up dating services. "It was not a good thing in any way," he admits. "I was just lonely, and here was an easy way to spend an evening with a woman. If the sex wasn't all that great and I got bored, I could easily move along to the next person."

He didn't want Owen to figure out too much, so he would not bring someone home unless he felt he was "serious" about her. Still, each liaison seemed to go stale after six to nine months. "Now I see that I was afraid of commitment. I'd never had any guidance about these things."

It was during this era that Mark's taste for pornography grew. He would occasionally buy movies or magazines, but he preferred the live atmosphere of strip clubs instead. By 2008, online porn became an every-night diversion. And then, he'd check in every morning before work, too. He schooled himself to be careful not to access

His appetite for stimulation kept escalating. He rationalized to himself, "I'm not hurting anybody."

photos of underage women, knowing that could get him in legal trouble. But his appetite for stimulation kept escalating.

He rationalized to himself, *I'm not hurting anybody.* Of course, he was badly neglecting his growing son. The boy would want to do something with his dad, only to hear, "Nah, I'm busy here at the computer ... maybe in a little while."

Then Mark began to wonder, *Wow—what would it have been like if I'd had the Internet back when I was a teenager?* He yearned to retrieve that early buzz. He began typing the words "teen porn" into the search boxes on his screen.

On November 5, 2010—a Friday—he came home from work to a quiet house; Owen was spending the weekend with his mother. Mark went straight to his computer and pulled up Craigslist to check the "Personals" section for possible new contacts. The screen loaded up ... and just then, there was a knock at the door. He went to answer it.

Busted

There stood a petite woman he didn't recognize. But suddenly, she held out a badge and announced, "I'm Detective Brenda Scott from the St. Cloud Police Department. May I talk to you?"

Mark caught his breath. She wasn't wearing a police uniform—but then, detectives seldom do. "Yeah, I guess," he finally mumbled. "Come on in."

She stepped into the entryway and said, "Your son apparently saw something on your computer about teenage porn, which is a felony. He told his mother, who contacted the Department of Human Services. So I'm here to investigate."

"Look, ma'am—I haven't done anything illegal," Mark hastened to explain. "Anything I've looked at ... they were all eighteen, nineteen years old or more."

"Well, that's what the websites often claim," the detective replied, "but that doesn't mean they're telling the truth. Would you mind if I looked at your computer?"

"Uh, sure. Come ahead."

Mark watched nervously as the woman worked the keyboard and mouse for a number of minutes. Not finding what she was looking for, she said she would need to take the computer in for more investigation. Mark nodded okay.

"I didn't know what to say or do. I was totally lost…. The minute she left my house, I tried to call my ex-wife and ask her why she would do this. She wouldn't answer.

"Not till the next day did I get through to her. We had a long talk. I proclaimed my innocence of doing anything illegal, but I did admit that I'd checked out other stuff that probably wasn't the best."

His ex had, over the past year or so, started coming to Hosanna, and bringing along Owen, now thirteen, when possible. She boldly said on the phone, "Well, the first place you need to go, Mark, is to church. They even have a prayer chapel there where you can get help and they have a program called Celebrate Recovery."

Twenty-four hours later, Mark was sitting in a row listening to me preach. I spoke about new life in Christ, and how baptism was a sign of burying the old and rising to a fresh beginning. (In fact, this was the same Sunday I mentioned in the earlier chapter about Max, the young man with Down syndrome—the day we offered baptisms at the atrium fountain.) Mark was touched with the hope that he could be forgiven. He got in line with the rest that morning.

He remembers seeing Owen moments later. "I'm so sorry for what I've done," he blurted out. "I think I need to go to the prayer room now."

"Can I go with you, Dad?" Owen asked with eyes wide.

"Sure." The two of them walked into the large room with couches and subdued lighting, where gentle instrumental music played in the background. A husband-and-wife team came to meet them.

Today, Mark can hardly speak through the tears as he describes what happened next. "To hear my thirteen-year-old son tell me in front of others that he forgave me ... it was overwhelming. I just totally broke down. I'd never really felt true forgiveness before. When they finished praying for me, I had this sense of being fifty pounds lighter."

Mark went over to his ex-wife's house that afternoon, where the three of them had a long talk. He wanted Owen to know that, despite the occasional on-screen pop-ups offering variant sex, he was not a homosexual. "But mostly, I just wanted to tell him how sorry I was that he even had to be aware of such a thing. Here I had grown up not wanting to be like my dad—and I was!"

His ex-wife looked Mark squarely in the eye and said, "I forgive you." She was a different person because of God in her life and I wanted what I saw.

A couple of weeks later, the police detective got in touch to say that no actual criminal evidence had shown up, so Mark could come get his computer.

"No, thanks!" he replied. "You made me realize my addiction. I've already canceled my Internet service."

"Well, we can't keep your private property," she explained. "You're going to have to do something with it." Mark ended up giving it to his ex-wife, who needed it. To this day, Mark does not have a computer at home.

"Yes, there are still temptations," he admits. "But I haven't watched or purchased any porn since that weekend. I haven't been to a single strip club or set up any meetings over the phone. It's like one of the speakers at Hosanna said: 'Don't look at negative events in your life as setbacks. View them as *set-ups* for what God will do in your future.'

"I actually feel love in this church—something I never felt before. I feel forgiven. Every time there's Communion, I get emotional, because I actually believe now that Jesus died for me and the stupid things I've done.

"Why would he do that? Because he loves me."

The Cost

Mark's story shows us the horrible cost of letting the fire get outside the fireplace. His addictions cost him his military career, his marriage, and his reputation. He almost lost his relationship with his son. When you hear the word *cost,* you usually think in terms of price. A dollar amount is assigned to determine the value or cost of something. But there are losses beyond value. You don't think in terms of dollars, but rather devastation.

A pastor who knows from personal experience says, "Sexual addiction is so time-consuming. It just drains the best of you." Here the loss is not only measured in hours and productivity, but in diminished character. The addiction gets the best of you. Your loved ones or your job get the left-overs. Integrity, honesty, and compassion are all compromised, if they exist at all. Your grasp of reality continues to erode as you slip further into denial.

As with any addiction, something has a hold on you. It steals your freedom as it sucks the life out of you. There is always a progression as the monster's appetite continues to grow. More time, more money, more lies are required. What once might have been a passing interest is now a possessive interest. It owns you.

The progression from soft-core to hard-core is well documented, as the bars on your personal prison gain strength. You are disgusted at what you see even as you are driven to see more.

Here's the biggest lie of all. Mark said it, and every sexual addict has used the same rationalization: *"I'm not hurting anybody.* It's just me and this computer screen. She chose to pose for this, probably got paid for it. I'm not physically touching or harming anyone. What's the big deal?"

Quite simply, at some level I think pornography is harmful to every female on the face of the planet. The addict objectifies women. He sees body parts, not the whole person. He has no interest in who she is, where she lives, or if anybody cares about her. His thoughts are impure and he is 100 percent self-absorbed.

This becomes the way he sees women in general—not always, but often. He undresses them in his mind and, once again, his selfish imagination fires up. That's why we have the word *leering,* and why the Bible says that to lust for a woman is to commit adultery in your heart (Matthew 5:28). President Jimmy Carter once quoted the Bible accurately in this regard,

> *Any addiction steals your freedom as it sucks the life out of you. There is always a progression as the monster's appetite continues to grow.*

and the ignorance and insolence of many American males were revealed. They skewered him for such an old-fashioned thought, even though he has spoken a timeless and divine truth.

Who Is She, Really?

This gets very personal for me and should for every man, if he thinks about it. I have a beautiful wife, a lovely daughter, and two adorable grand-daughters. They mean the world to me; they bring charm and grace and joy to any setting or occasion. I would like for them to be seen by all men as amazing, intelligent, gifted, and loved. But as long as pornography abounds, that will not be the case.

What's more, there is an element of privilege or even ownership to pornography. The man feels he has a right to look and fantasize. He's paid for the right and she's made herself available. The problem is that these feelings are then brought into real-life relationships. When the woman resists or denies what he feels he is entitled to, violence follows. Does anyone really claim that no one gets hurt in all of this?

When I preach or teach on this topic at Hosanna, I challenge men to see other women—all other women—the same way they want their wives or daughters to be seen by other men. I remind them that the woman in any picture or on any screen is *someone's daughter.* She may also be someone's wife or even a mom. She is almost certainly not there by choice. If men want their daughters to be respected and admired, that's how they need to treat women.

In this chapter, I have chosen not to research or write about the drug addiction and prostitution that are almost always a part of the pornography industry. Those facts and statistics are readily available, and the cost to our country is unimaginable. The violence, brokenness, abuse, sickness, incarceration, and death that come with prostitution have to make one shudder when the lie is repeated ... *I'm not hurting anyone.*

I admit there's not much humor in this chapter and it sounds kind of "preachy." You might even think I'm a prude. I think so too sometimes, but I obviously have strong feelings on this topic. So does the Bible. "Run away from sexual sin! No other sin so clearly affects the body as this one does. For sexual immorality is a sin against your own body."[34]

So I'll just give you some more ammunition for that prude thought. I used to love reading *Sports Illustrated.* I'll write another book someday about all of my athletic accomplishments. Actually, it will be a short story. Fiction mostly. But I always liked the writers of *SI,* and in the past—the way past—Minnesota actually had some teams that were written about. Have you ever heard of Kirby Puckett? So there.

Then the *Sports Illustrated* swimsuit edition started coming. You had to rationalize this one a little bit, but if you liked to swim or play beach volleyball it made sense for all of us good sports. So let's just keep this dirty little secret among us boys. Except it is no secret.

Every man who has looked at the swimsuit edition knows exactly where his eyes and his thoughts go. And the thought is NOT, "Gee, my wife would look good in that." So I canceled my subscription many years back. I didn't want the temptation to come right into my house. Prude. I suppose so, because I also wrote to Victoria's Secret and asked that their catalogs not come to my address. Plus, I just didn't know what some of those women were wearing and I didn't want to ask anybody.

Here's another wild thought—are you still reading? I don't walk around with my eyes shut. I do notice women. And of all the things that God created, including Trunk Bay on St. John (the most beautiful beach in the world, says National Geographic), women are by far his best work in terms of beauty, intrigue, complexity, movement, elegance, and wow. So, when I see a beautiful woman I bring a simple thought into my mind. A simple prayer actually: "Nice work, God!" If I'm congratulating him, I'm not objectifying her. It's amazing how neat and orderly your thoughts can be when you invite God into the living room of your mind.

"Fix your thoughts on what is true and honorable and right. Think about things that are pure and lovely and admirable. Think about things that are excellent and worthy of praise."[35] That verse helps when there are pretty women around, or you're getting your butt kicked in squash. (One of my athletic accomplishments.)

Crawl Toward the Daylight

One of the men who talked to me gave a graphic description of the addiction itself and what it took to get out of it. "I had to be willing to be put into a narrow place. Think of crawling through a sewer conduit on your hands and knees, in your own vomit or excrement. If you're not crawling forward, you're probably getting sick and stuck and scared. But if you look toward the other end, people are waiting for you. My wife kept waiting for me even though she was angry. I understand that. She had every right to be."

> *The woman in any picture or on any screen is <u>someone's daughter.</u>*

Mark expressed the two key elements to getting out: confession and forgiveness. Confession means you admit you have a problem, you're ready to get some help and to be held accountable. You want to put the fire back into the fireplace. Forgiveness brings cleansing. We talk about "dirty" movies or "dirty" magazines—the need for cleansing is obvious.

Not surprisingly the Bible describes this path to freedom. "If we say we have no sin, we are only fooling ourselves and refusing to accept the truth. But if we confess our sins to him, he is faithful

219

and just to forgive us and to cleanse us from every wrong."[36]

God's desire is for our freedom and for us to be in a full, life-giving relationship with him. I said that the woman is *someone's daughter*. You are also *Someone's son*. That's the truth. And the truth will always set you free.

12

BEYOND ALL REASON

I'm a reasonable person.

I have left some blank space for those who know me to write in their own rebuttal. Nancy will need more space. What I mean to say is that I am a rational, thinking person. When I do those thinking-style inventories, it shows that I am a Concrete Sequential thinker. I like to think solid thoughts (things that make sense), and I like to line those thoughts up in a logical sequence. Obviously, this is how everyone should think.

My wife is an Abstract Random thinker. Honestly, with my Concrete Sequential mind, I can't even describe how her brain works. The closest I can come is this: Have you ever been hit on the head so hard that you saw stars? For a while those "stars" just float in and out of your vision. It seems to me that Nancy's thoughts are like that much of the time. They just float around, in, and out of her mind, and every once in a while she grabs one. But not for long, because another beauty soon comes along.

I fully realize that all this makes me sound arrogant and superior. The truth is, one of the biggest reasons I married Nancy and I need her is her random, spontaneous, free-flowing mind. She's the hit at parties, not me. She's always at the center of the laughter and stories. They usually ask me to go out and buy more chips. I admire the way she sees the world. Most of the time.

So for me, there are some things that seem unreasonable or beyond reason. Things like the New York Yankees winning another pennant, or getting patted down (groped) at the airport, or January in Minnesota. These things don't make sense to me.

Perhaps nothing is more unreasonable than the death of a child. Hope, a marvelous future, innocence, joy, curiosity all extinguished prematurely. Who can make sense of that? Who can find any reason for that to happen? Now, there has been an abrupt change in the tone and feel of this chapter. I just want to prepare you for what is to come.

This is a chapter about sorrow and loss. Most of us think these are to be avoided. Most of us also know that isn't possible, or even reasonable. As much as we like to escape with our books, movies, trips, and games, the reality of sorrow usually returns—and when we least expect it. Jesus, who spoke the truth and was himself the Truth, said, "Here on earth you will have many trials and sorrows."[37] He wanted us to be prepared for all the realities of life.

Go Figure

There is a story about sorrow and loss in the Bible. It's not just a chapter, it's a whole book about it—the Book of Job (it's pronounced with a long *o*, like *robe*). The story starts with Job being described as "blameless—a man of complete integrity. He feared God and stayed away from evil." Job was one of the good guys. You should also know that "he was, in fact, the richest person in that entire area." So far, so good.

However, one day God and Satan were having a discussion (it's in the book). And God said, "Have you noticed my servant Job?" He went on to brag about what a good man he was. Satan's response was "Yes, Job fears you, but *not without good reason.*" Essentially Satan went on to say Job probably wouldn't be so wonderful and God-fearing if he wasn't living the lifestyle of the rich and famous.

God then allowed Satan to test Job. He could do anything he wanted to him, short of killing him. This is when the sorrow and loss began. Job lost everything, all of his animals and his possessions, and all of his children died. Then he broke out with a horrible case of boils all over his body. His wife had some wonderful advice for him: "Curse God and die." Thank you, darling.

It turns into a long story. Three friends show up and start to give Job all kinds of advice and counsel. One after the other they try to explain why all this was happening to Job. They assume there must be reasons for all these events, and they were more than ready to spell them out. To be clear, no one has ever proved that The Three Stooges were based on this trio, but one has to wonder.

Finally, God shows up in chapter 38. He speaks to Job from a whirlwind, which means he was pretty stirred up. God fires dozens of questions at Job: "Where were you when I laid the foundations of the earth? Who defined the boundaries of the sea? Do you know where the gates of death are located? Where is the path to the origin of light?" On and on, the questions just keep coming. Job realizes how futile and puny his knowledge truly is. He repents of all his own questions and doubts ... and the Lord restores his fortunes. "In fact, the Lord gave him twice as much as before!" So all ends well.

But what if the story had stopped after chapter 41? The unanswerable questions had all been asked, but the restoration had not yet taken place. I know a couple who are living between chapters 41 and 42. They've experienced significant loss, and so many of their questions have no answers. But their faith and resilience will amaze you. And, I hope, inspire you.

All-American Family

Brian and Katy Coatney didn't have children right away after their marriage in 1976; in fact, they couldn't. They prayed earnestly about this, and eventually they met an unlikely source of advice. Brian was a U.S. Marine pilot, and a fellow officer's wife (who was Chinese) said she could solve the problem through acupuncture. Believe what you will about that methodology—the Coatneys had three kids within five years! Brennan was the first to arrive, followed by his sister Bridgette, and finally another boy named Kellen.

The family eventually settled back here in the Twin Cities and found a good church in Bloomington. The children thrived in the youth programs. "Bridgette got a bunch of her school friends to come over every Wednesday night for pizza," Katy remembers, "and then we'd drive the whole gang to church. All of those girls made commitments to Jesus during that time." The key verse of the junior high group in those years was Jeremiah 29:11—"'For I know the plans I have for you,' says the Lord. 'They are plans for good and not for disaster, to give you a future and a hope.'"

Kellen, the youngest, enjoyed church as well, even though he could be a little edgy at times. He came home from summer youth camp one year, for example, with a pierced ear. When he started his freshman year of high school, something ugly happened after a football game that the parents didn't know about for several weeks. Kellen and some of his friends were pitching rocks at cars passing by. A friend hit one, and the car screeched to a halt. Out jumped two seniors, who had been drinking.

They proceeded to catch Kellen and beat him up. Then, for a crowning insult, they urinated on him. At school the next week, it made for a colorful story, which quickly went viral through the halls.

"Bridgette caught wind of it," Brian says, "and when she clued us in, we were horrified. A whole campaign of humiliation took root, turning Kellen's year into a nightmare. The only friends willing to associate with him seemed to be 'loser' types. That was about the time Kellen started using marijuana.

"And then it escalated to methamphetamines. It was a very difficult, dark time for our family."

Pressing Restart

In desperation, Brian and Katy decided they'd need to switch school systems, which is what brought them here to Lakeville. They began seeking out various treatment programs for their troubled son. He would spend two weeks away at a residential facility ... only to relapse when he came home. Three-week plans, full-month plans—none seemed to turn him around.

At one point he was required to do some "community service." His high school counselor had no ready programs at hand but said, "There's a good church here in Lakeville called Hosanna. They'll take anybody!" And soon, the young man was doing custodial work around our campus, building sets for the Easter production, cleaning windows. We tried our best to be warm and affirming toward him.

Understandably, the parents and sister started checking us out on Sundays (Brennan, the oldest, was out of the house by now). They found Hosanna to be a refuge in their storm. Family counseling helped as well, giving them a picture of the dynamics at home. "We all had to grow up," says Brian. "It was as if we were all working hard to 'save Kellen,'" who nevertheless was spending more time on the streets than at home.

Another six-month rehab program up in Bemidji did not stabilize him any more than the earlier attempts. "We were getting nervous," says Katy. "If you're going to 'intervene' with someone's behavior, you have to act before they turn eighteen. We really felt we had only one last shot." They selected a year-long program at a highly endorsed psychiatric program for troubled teens called Peninsula Village, outside Knoxville, Tennessee.

But how would they ever get their son to go that far away. Desperate, they resorted to subterfuge. Katy worked for Northwest Airlines (now Delta), and so the family was used to flying stand-by for free, which meant odd routes. At the end of a California vacation, Brian and his son flew homeward via Memphis, a Northwest hub—but then connected onward to Knoxville. "I bought him a *Sports Illustrated* to distract him," Brian admits. "We came out of the airport, jumped into a cab, and I gave the driver a note that said, *Peninsula Village—don't say a word.*"

The cab eventually pulled up to a nice hotel-style complex, where an administrator waited outside. Opening the door, he said, "Welcome, Kellen. It's good to meet you. You'll need to say goodbye to your dad now, because you're not going to be seeing him for a while."

Kellen gasped with shock at what was happening. Dropping to the ground, he moaned, "But I was doing so good!"

A Breakthrough

During that year (2005-06), teachers encouraged him; a psychiatrist finally diagnosed his OCD (obsessive-compulsive disorder) and put him on the right medications. Two young staffers—former gang members—talked to him about Jesus. Kellen saw that he could still actually have a future. He gave his heart to the Lord.

At graduation, he was named class valedictorian. His grades had improved enough for him to think about college. He came home a promising young man of eighteen. He made peace with Bridgette, who had resented the disruption he had caused in the family. He even got a tattoo on his back of the Beatitudes—in Hebrew, no less!

The next year was spent working on his sobriety. He wanted to apply to Winona State University, a school of 8,500 students two hours' drive down the Mississippi River. "We were a little concerned about that," says Brian. "We had hoped he'd choose something closer to home, with more of a Christian environment. But—he was eighteen, after all."

When he checked in for the fall semester of 2007, he at least avoided dorm life, opting instead for a tiny top-floor apartment he found through a widow at the local Alcoholics Anonymous meeting. The parents held their breath. Bridgette moved out to start nursing school in Detroit, rooming with two other girls, and working in an upscale restaurant. Her grades, as always, were superior. Was everybody on a good path now, Brian and Katy wondered?

"Kellen came home the following summer— and started relapsing right in front of us," they said. "The environment down at Winona had not been good for him. His answers to our questions were vague. We could tell he didn't care about his future once again. We were pretty terrified.

"But he insisted on going back for his sophomore year. We arranged for some counseling down there for him."

In December, he got picked up by the police on a DUI. Since he was under twenty-one, there was zero tolerance; he lost his driver's license.

Then came the Friday night of March 7, 2009, when "we got the call that every parent dreads," Brian relates in a soft voice. "He had been out with some friends drinking ... they got up on a roof ... and he fell off. He was now on life support in the hospital.

"We rushed down to Winona. But we never really got a chance to speak with him. He lay there unconscious, with massive brain trauma ... we finally had to let him go."

It was one of the hardest funerals I've ever had to conduct. "I am sure you are asking today," I said, "the question 'So where was God last Friday night?'" I tried to persuade those gathered that God had never taken his eye off Kellen, not for a moment ... that this was not part of his plan or his will. "God is a God of life," I said, "and I'm absolutely certain that his were the first tears shed." Then I added, "May I gently remind everyone in the room that God knows the pain and sorrow of having a son die."

Staring into Fog

As Brian and Katy talk, the agony of their loss—especially after so much effort, so many rescue attempts—engulfs the room. They do not rant or castigate; they mostly stare at the floor. An observer can hardly imagine the pain that throbs within them.

Finally, Brian speaks again. "We came to church the next Sunday, but couldn't even make ourselves go into the service. We just wanted to sit out in the atrium and drink coffee.... In the bulletin, though, we saw something about GriefShare, 'a support group for people experiencing the loss of someone close.' We decided to try it out."

Here in this circle, Brian and Katy met other parents who had lost children, and were a little further along in their healing process. It gave them hope. The Bible study dealt with the subject of heaven, which was a comfort. The facilitators were kind and gentle as they surrounded the couple with love.

"We gradually began to think we could have a life again," Katy says with a faint smile. "I talked with Bridgette a lot by phone about what we were learning." The daughter actually had another uplifting topic to add to the conversation. She had met the love of her life, a fine young man there in Detroit named Nick.

In November, he proposed. A wedding to plan! What better balm for Katy's torn and tattered soul. Things got even better when one of Bridgette's regular customers at the high-end restaurant offered her a $6,000 designer wedding dress that was left behind when their own daughter's plans had fallen apart.

In April, Bridgette came home for six weeks of planning with her mother. They reveled in the flurry of color and menu selections, flower choices and program designs. As Memorial Day neared, she returned to Detroit.

The next day, while doing laundry over at Nick's house, she suddenly fainted. A family member called 9-1-1 just as Nick was arriving home from his job. An ambulance rushed Bridgette to the hospital. When she regained consciousness, she revealed that she'd had a fainting spell the day before, too, in the Minneapolis airport, but hadn't told anyone.

"We jumped on a plane," Brian says, "and got to her side as quickly as we could. Over the weekend, she seemed to be doing better. Lots of visitors from school and the restaurant came to see her, which lifted her spirits. There wasn't a clear diagnosis, however. What was going on?"

On Monday, Memorial Day, the parents returned home to reorganize so they could then take turns caring for their daughter in Detroit— Mom on certain days, Dad in between. Tuesday brought the news that Bridgette was feeling well enough to be discharged. "Okay," said Katy, "I'm coming back tomorrow. I can't get there tonight, though."

"That's okay, Mama. My roommates will take care of me. I'll see you then."

At GriefShare that night, Katy couldn't get Bridgette out of her mind. She phoned immediately after the meeting. "How are you doing, honey?"

"Okay—I just got back home," she replied. "I'm awfully tired...."

"I love you, sweetheart. I'll see you tomorrow."

"I love you, Mama."

At 8:50 the next morning, as Katy sat at work trying to clear her desk in order to fly out for Detroit at noon—the phone rang. Bridgette was gone! It turned out there was a serious clot in her lung, possibly the result of having recently started birth control pills in anticipation of the coming marriage. But maybe not ... no cause was ever determined.

A Boatload of Questions

The blow of losing two-thirds of their offspring within fifteen months has rocked the Coatneys unimaginably. It makes no sense. Why should any couple have to absorb such calamity, especially when they had tried with all their might and resources throughout the years to be good parents?

"We don't know why this happened," Brian says in a flat tone. "We've read a lot of books about heaven recently, for sure. I'm not sure what God has in store for us now. But we'll get a chance to ask him our questions someday. And then it will all make perfect sense."

Katy adds: "When you lose children, you almost live in fear of questions about your family. It's just natural for the casual person to say, 'Do you have kids?' You don't want to overwhelm them with too much information. I finally came up with this answer: 'Yes—I have two kids in heaven, and one who lives in St. Paul!'

"We'll get a chance to ask God our questions someday. And then it will all make perfect sense."

"We're trying to figure out what our life is going to be now. But I don't feel bitter. I'm not angry. Thanks to GriefShare, I feel cared for. I have to honestly say, though, that I would like some answers."

Theirs is a story not yet finished.

You probably would agree with me that what Brian and Katy have experienced is beyond all reason. It's not logical, it's not fair, it doesn't make sense. For many people this is a huge barrier to faith. Their idea is: If there is a God, life will be fair. He'll see to it. Why wouldn't he, if he is all-powerful and all-knowing? So, when outrageous, painful, unfair things happen to very good people, that's proof enough for them that there is no God. At least not the kind of God you'd want to believe in and trust.

Why don't the Coatneys feel that way? They have more justification than any other couple I know. And yet, they remain people of faith, hope, confidence, and even joy. Is it then a false hope or a manufactured faith? Are they are living in some kind of denial? Has their overwhelming grief numbed them to reality? Absolutely not.

They do still grieve for Kellen and Bridgette, and they will for as long as they live. But in the midst of that grief they continue to look to the Author of Life even when there has been loss of life. They are reasonable people who have a firm grasp on reality, but in that reality they see a Resurrection, and it makes all the difference in the world. Their world. This world.

I quoted Jesus as this chapter began: "Here on earth you will have many trials and sorrows". The very next thing he said was this: *"But take heart, because I have overcome the world."*[38] It sounds like something Superman would say (a silly comment that the editors will probably delete). It actually sounds like something only a Savior could say, one who has fully entered into our world and experienced the pain, sorrow, testing, and trial that we experience. And the death. Somehow, he overcame it all. He defeated anything that would defeat us, and he makes promises that can shape our thoughts, our hopes, and our future.

Coming Our Direction

Here's the deal. Almost 700 years before Jesus was born it was predicted—the Bible word is

235

"prophesied"—that such a rescuer would come. One of those predictions can be found in Isaiah 53. It's one of the most amazing chapters in the Bible because it perfectly describes who Jesus would be and what would happen to him. He would suffer horribly and die, all according to "the Lord's good plan."[39]

Why should that concern you? Two reasons.

First, out of all the major world religions, only Christianity describes God so fully entering into our world, our geography, our issues, our flesh. There's a fancy word for it—*incarnation.* It means "wrapped in flesh." That's how Jesus came. I just want to point that out, because a prevailing drumbeat these days is that all religions lead to God. No one religion should get all arrogant or exclusive, claiming it has the truth.

> *It's not arrogant or exclusive to point out that only one religion describes God coming to us.*

It's not arrogant or exclusive to point out that only one religion describes God *coming to us.* That is one of the unique and distinguishing things about Christianity. It's worth knowing, not to win arguments, but because of what Jesus said: "Here on earth *you will* have many trials and sorrows. But take heart, because *I have* overcome the world." What you will experience relates directly to what he has done.

That's the second reason why all this is so important. It's personal. It's not just religion or theology or history. It relates to your Monday world and all that will come your way. Because Jesus experienced hunger, loneliness, anger, sorrow, rejection, and death, he understands us. He knows us. More than that, he has overcome these life-stealing events. He has faced them, stood up to them, prevailed, and provided us the way to do the same. That's the very reason he came—to show us how to live, now and forever. Amen.

I wrote the "Amen" because the last three or four paragraphs sound pretty much like a sermon. Some of you almost dozed off or started counting ceiling tiles. I simply don't know another way to describe what's going on with the Coatneys. They have faith. Faith is not another word for hope or belief. "Faith is the confidence that what we hope for will actually happen; it gives us assurance about things we cannot see."[40] To stand on faith is to stand on very solid ground. To have faith is to have assurance. This doesn't just "keep them going" through pain and sorrow. It actually removes the pain and sorrow and replaces it with the promises of eternity with a gracious God and all believers.

For Real?

A popular book just now is entitled *Heaven Is for Real* by Todd Burpo. It tells of a four-year-old boy who was critically sick after his appendix had burst. Once he recovered, he began volunteering lengthy, detailed, amazing, extraordinary accounts of his time in heaven.

He saw angels, talked with Jesus, and met his grandfather. He also met his little sister—who had miscarried and who had never been mentioned to the boy up to that point. What this family experienced has become their clearest, greatest reality, making their earthly experience seem a bit unreal and certainly only temporary.

Now this book could all just be some fine bedtime reading, or a good way to ignore the strange guy next to you on a plane. Some people would place these books in the fiction category. The thing is, they perfectly support and confirm the most important promises given to us in the Bible concerning heaven and eternal life.

- The promise of eternal life has been given to all who believe in Jesus Christ. "Everyone who believes in him will not perish but have eternal life."[41]

- Heaven is beyond stunning, beyond our human imagination. "No eye has seen, no ear has heard, and no mind has imagined what God has prepared for those who love him."[42]

- We will be fully present with God. "Yes, we are fully confident, and we would rather be away from these bodies, for then we will be at home with the Lord."[43]

- A place has been prepared and is waiting for us. "Don't let your hearts be troubled. Trust in God, and trust also in me. There is more than enough room in my Father's home.... When everything is ready, I will come and get you, so that you will always be with me where I am."[44]

- Maybe this is the best part for those who are feeling their age, or they put a tattoo in the wrong place, or they're too short (like me): We get new bodies! Brand-new, not low-mileage. *No* mileage. "For we know that when this earthly tent we live in is taken down (that is, when we die and leave this earthly body), we will have a house in heaven, an eternal body made for us by God himself and not by human hands."[45]

There are many more promises in the Bible, but you've got the idea. This is going to be better than a trip to the Grand Canyon or a little nip and tuck on the bulges and wrinkles. As I said, these promises shape our thoughts, our hopes, and our future. We don't live in waiting. Life now is not about escape to a better environment. We are comforted now because of promises made. We are confident now because of faith given. We are happy and hopeful now because of what waits for us.

I mentioned earlier that the Job story ended well. Chapter 42 tells us that all of Job's wealth was restored (actually, doubled). He was even given a new family.

Brain and Katy are living at the end of Chapter 41. They have the promises that, for them, Chapter 42 will come. There will be a family reunion, a healing of broken hearts, and a joy beyond the telling.

Meanwhile (such a hard word) they live with unanswered questions:

Why did these things happen?
How could God allow them?
Did he cause them?
How can I trust him anymore?

Each question is weighty. Each begs for an answer. And, each tears at the fabric of faith.

But faith is not based on knowledge, at least not knowledge as we think of it: knowing facts and having answers. Faith is based on knowing the One who has all the answers. "Fear of the Lord is the foundation of true knowledge."[46]

Would you rather have a God who explains himself or reveals himself? That choice is clear, because God has already made it for us. Through his Word, written and in the flesh (Jesus), God has revealed his heart. It's a heart filled with grace, mercy, patience, and love for me. And for you.

That's the knowledge that I need. Knowing that, knowing him, is my anchor and my hope.

I used to think that knowing led to believing. If you knew enough and you got your questions answered, you'd cross the line and become a believer. I almost didn't go into the ministry because I thought pastors had to have all the answers—and I knew I didn't. Now, I realize that believing leads to knowledge.

In the fullness of time Brian and Katy will get all their questions answered. Meanwhile (maybe that word isn't so hard) they know the One who has all the answers. They trust him, and that's enough.

For me, this is not beyond reason. "The Spirit is God's guarantee that *he will give us the inheritance he promised* and that he has purchased us to be his own people. He did this so we would praise and glorify him."[47]

Conclusion

MONDAY MONDAY

Since you have read this entire book, I picture you as a savvy and intelligent reader. Either that or you are one of my relatives and you felt obligated to slog through this whole thing because you know we are going to bump into each other at Christmastime. Either way, as a person of intelligence and/or good DNA, you certainly realize that the very best music ever written and sung comes out of the late 1960s.

Come on. The Lovin' Spoonful. The Dave Clark Five. Early Simon and Garfunkel. It makes me cry to even think about it. Chad and Jeremy. That music told a story about love or cars or surfing. Think Beach Boys. The Beatles were fabulous until they all climbed aboard their yellow submarine, then nobody wanted to hold their hand. I don't know if they broke up or sank first. Today the closest thing to sixties music is country, but that slide thing they play gives me vertigo, and how many drinking songs are really worth listening to?

Don't forget Petula Clark, The Four Tops, The Doors, and CCR. Where's the Kleenex?

Anyway, one of my all-time favorite songs is "Monday Monday" by the Mamas and the Papas. A little moody, kinda sad, good harmony, love lost. (Did Mama Cass really die eating a sandwich? Some stories just don't go away.) They sing with regret because Monday has come. "Monday Monday, can't trust that day." Coming off the weekend, the feelings were good on Monday morning, but she was gone by Monday evening. "But whenever Monday comes, you find me cryin' all of the time." That song takes me back to all the times Nancy and I broke up. Love is never easy. Where's the Kleenex?

Here's the deal: Monday has always gotten a bad rap. There aren't any TGIM restaurants across America. No dress-casual Mondays. They even took Monday Night Football and moved it to Sunday night. For cryin' out loud, Howard Cosell almost came back from the grave and, if you sit still, you can tap your memory bank and hear Dandy Don singing, "The party's over...." Monday comes in seventh on My Favorite Day surveys every time.

Somehow this Mondays-are-miserable mindset has crept into our thinking about God. I know a lot of pastors who take Mondays off. All that preaching on the weekend can wear a guy out, and the tee times are wide open on Mondays.

Fine, but that doesn't mean that God takes Mondays off. I hope we've discovered in these pages that somehow God got out of church. I don't know who let him out, but he's on the loose. The calendar doesn't seem to faze him one bit. He's out there showing compassion, bringing conviction, and building character seven days a week. Maybe Motel 6 stole their motto from him: *We'll leave the light on for ya.*

And it seems like God does some of his best work on the weekdays, even Monday. Last Monday night we started our Partnership Class again at Hosanna. (We used to call them Membership Classes, but when you are a member, you have to pay dues. Think tennis club. When you are a partner, you invest. Think stakeholder.)

So, we had just started the class and there were about 120 people in the room. Most didn't know each other. Their eyes were fixed on the agenda or some bug on the floor. I greeted them and said we should start our time together in some dangerous, outrageous fashion. Now, eyes were on me and thoughts of cutting class were beginning to simmer.

I simply said that if anyone had a God encounter in their Monday world, they should raise their hand and tell us about it. I added that if your heart was beating fast, that was a good sign you had something to say. A couple of hands went up right away. Here's what one young woman said:

I wasn't sure if I should come tonight. I've been coming to Hosanna for five years and felt guilty for not joining, but my schedule is crazy. As my six-year-old daughter was eating her breakfast this morning, she told me that she had a dream about me last night. She pictured me sitting at a table with a group of people and then, all of the sudden, I was standing up talking to the whole group. When I was done, they all clapped for me and I cried because I was so happy. I knew I was supposed to come tonight.

She finished, sat down, and we all clapped. Doesn't the Bible say something about God speaking to us through visions and dreams, and that we have to have the faith of a child to enter the kingdom of God?

Another woman volunteered:

I was working at Starbucks this afternoon when three of our machines broke down, and for the next hour everybody who came in got free coffee. The mood is always good there, but I've never seen so much laughter and conversation. People loved drinking their free coffee. And, since they couldn't pay for it, they left some wonderful tips. I just think God wanted to bless those people.

She sat down and we clapped again.

The Bible tells us again and again that God's grace is free and unmerited. We can't pay for it, can't earn it. It's his gift to us. But it's a game changer. We sing "Amazing Grace" because grace is amazing. It changes our attitude and outlook, our direction and destiny. When people fully receive such a gift, they do want to talk about it and spread the joy.

In our Partnership Class, there was already a connection and some excitement in the room. I believe this is one of the best ways for the church to build faith—any church. It happens when people are willing to take a risk, with hearts pounding, standing in front of strangers. They tell a little story of a touch from God. Others lean in, faith is strengthened, and God draws closer. It's not that he was so far away, but he uses such messengers and storytellers to build our faith. And faith always improves our vision and our hearing. Faith is our capacity to see God at work and hear his voice.

God of Our Mondays

Now, I'm not saying you should shout "Praise God" when you get more sprinkles on your donut than I do. I don't like sprinkles that much and I wanted you to have that one. Or, when you are late for an appointment and the parking spot *right by the door* opens just as you pull up. That may be a sign of God's favor—or the guy leaving may be a burglar speeding off in the getaway car.

The point is, I don't think God arranges the dust on the coffee table in any particular pattern, but I do believe that he is God of circumstances. We often encourage people to see coincidences as

God-incidences. Oftentimes (not always) God arranges little surprises or interruptions to bless us, show us something, or rescue us. The God who numbers the hairs on your head and knows the stars by name can do that.

Our *sophistication* gets in the way of enjoying some of God's gifts. Because we understand the earth's orbit around the sun, we might take a glorious sunset for granted. Because we understand the rise and fall of the tides, we may take for granted the billions of shells God so freely offers on the shores of Sanibel Island.

Our *schedules* get in the way of enjoying some of God's gifts. Our hurry can take us right past a child who may have a smile or a Kingdom insight for us. Our appointments and goals might squeeze out opportunities to hear the still small voice of the Almighty. Maybe he just wants to say, "You are the apple of my eye." But hurry hinders hearing.

Our *skepticism* gets in the way of enjoying some of God's gifts. When someone does something "nice" for us, we question their motives. When open-heart surgery becomes routine we just think that's what modern medicine is supposed to do. We don't see the healing hand of God.

Here's what I need to work on: Every Monday morning I make out a TDL—a To-Do List. (In some other chapter it was revealed that I actually make out four of these things, but I don't want to talk about that now.) I know my schedule at work and the things that need to get done around the house, so I list preparations and projects, to prioritize them and enjoy the profound satisfaction of crossing them off the list when completed. All of this can be analyzed, or Nancy can explain it to you.

What I need to do is also create a TBL—a To-Be List. I would do this, not to create order and take charge, but to create awareness and heighten expectation. Every week I should write stuff down like, "Be helpful," "Be bold," "Be kind," "Be quiet," and "Be ready." This would remind me that I am a human *being*, not a human *doing*. It would also give God greater opportunity to move about in my life and heart. I know he wants to surprise me and show me things. Busyness is not a very workable clay for him to shape. Beingness is. (When you're an author, you can make up your own words.)

Waiting and Working

My favorite Bible verse is Isaiah 40:31—"But those who wait on the Lord will find new strength. They will fly high on wings like eagles. They will run and not grow weary. They will walk and not faint." There is so much that I like about the strength and the flying and the running. Nancy and I walk often, and we find that some of the hills have gotten a little steeper, so even that last part sounds good. But it all flows out of waiting on the Lord.

When I was younger I understood that to mean that we are to wait, be patient. Then the Lord will give us the good stuff described in the verse. Psalm 46:10 says, "Be still and know that I am God!" I suppose that our heavenly Father is not unlike an earthly parent who sometimes needs to say, "Sit still." In the stillness God grants us rest, strength, and renewal. Our thoughts and senses can soar. I like that.

But, clearly there is a second and equally important meaning to "waiting on" the Lord. We are to serve him. And in serving we find a higher calling and an untapped strength. I'm quite certain that, sometimes, when we are waiting on the Lord (first meaning), he is waiting for us. Waiting for us to get off our duffs, get out of our pity party, get over our last setback, and get it in gear.

There's probably a better way to say all of that, but when the Lord was standing in front of over five thousand hungry people, he told his disciples, "You feed them."[48] What a scene. A hungry mob and twelve men who could catch fish and collect taxes, but were clueless about multiplication, even with the Master in their midst. I bet that happened on a Monday. It wasn't a time for waiting. It was a time for serving.

It's in a season of sorrow that we may well encounter the Messiah who wept. In a season of sacrifice, we come to know the Savior who gave his life. In the act of serving, we find ourselves shoulder to shoulder with One who said, "For even I, the Son of Man, came here not to be served but to serve others."[49] When we wait on the Lord (second meaning), we find ourselves walking with the Lord.

A missionary was describing Jesus to a primitive tribe. The chief interrupted and said, "We know who you are talking about. It's Dr. Morrow." This man had come years earlier to serve the people with medicine and compassion. He gave his life doing it, and so the people knew Jesus because of this faithful servant.

I wonder how often God comes along in circum-stances and through people, all quite normal and natural. And yet, there is something supernatural going on. God, in our town and in our time, accomplishing his will and purposes. Heaven touching earth. God, busy being God, even on a Monday.

So, we're back where we began. I said I wanted my thoughts about God to be my reality. I wanted the God that I worship on Sunday to show up on Monday. Turns out, he not only shows up, but he's got hopes and plans and work for me to do. You too.

I'm writing these last thoughts on a Sunday evening. I can't wait to see what God's up to tomorrow.

Endnotes

[1] Proverbs 3:5-6
[2] 1 Samuel 1:19 KJV
[3] Jeremiah 29:11
[4] Romans 8:28
[5] John 8:32
[6] Judges 14:6; 14:19; 15:14 (NLT 1996 edition)
[7] Jeremiah 31:16-17
[8] Luke 15:11-32
[9] 1 John 4:8
[10] John 8:1-11
[11] See Genesis 39:19-23
[12] Genesis 41:16
[13] John 8:32
[14] Mary J. Nelson, *Grace for Each Hour* (Minneapolis: Bethany, 2005), 43-44
[15] Psalm 84:10
[16] James 5:15-16, italics added
[17] Romans 8:28
[18] Psalm 55:1-8, 12-18, 20-23 NLT
[19] Joshua 7:5
[20] Psalm 31:4
[21] Psalm 35:7
[22] Psalm 57:6
[23] Matthew 5:44
[24] Colossians 3:19 (italics added)
[25] Psalm 91:1-2
[26] Genesis 8:22
[27] Revelation 21:5
[28] 1 Chronicles 28:20
[29] Deuteronomy 34:7
[30] Psalm 92:1, 2, 4, 10, 12, 14
[31] See Genesis 1:4, 10, 12, 18, 21, 25, 31
[32] See Genesis 2:18
[33] Genesis 2:23
[34] 1 Corinthians 6:18
[35] Philippians 4:8

36 1 John 1:8-9
37 John 16:33
38 John 16:33
39 Isaiah 53:10
40 Hebrews 11:1
41 John 3:16
42 1 Corinthians 2:9
43 2 Corinthians 5:8
44 John 14:1-3
45 2 Corinthians 5:1
46 Proverbs 1:7
47 Ephesians 1:14, italics added
48 Mark 6:37
49 Matthew 20:28